The Gospel According to Judas
A Handbook on Life

by

John H. Doe

Herald of The Lord Jesus Christ

a.k.a.

Sir Michael of the Candle

Knight of the Narrow Way

PROLOGUE

On February 20, 1974, science fiction author Philip K. Dick began a journey into an otherworldly state of being. He was no longer just writing about the fantastic, but entered an utterly strange, strangely compelling, far country of experience. He wrote that he felt the presence of a twin, whom he called Thomas, whom he thought must have lived in apostolic days. Many of his thoughts, which he did not neglect to put on paper, are scattered, almost confused, a man who was reaching beyond reality and trying to put the things he found in terms ill suited for such abstraction.

I understand his situation, more than anyone else: I *am* that Thomas, and I am in the world he inhabited in the last eight years of his life. I have been here a quarter of a century, with that world peeking in and sometimes taking over. I am the twin of Philip K. Dick, for I saw a cosmic egg split, a pink glow going away, and a blue glow entering me. He only saw the pink glow. I have a more developed, clearer picture than he did, for he laid down much groundwork in the years he was in it. I also have had more time to become accustomed to its environs. And here, I will relate my findings. My visions. The madness and the dreaming. This is my Gospel for to write.

I find I can make sense of things. Of heaven and earth, I can understand how things come to be, why things are, what must surely come. If, upon reading that, you decide to dismiss me off hand, I will not keep you. Only those who were meant to read on will. Just know that destiny is real, and it sometimes hangs upon on your choice. If you want to dismiss me, you must think that you have a better handle on things than I must have... or do you even care? True, you don't know me from Adam, but what if the crazy man's right? What if I show you that you do *not*, in fact, have a better grasp of what truly goes on? I try to say this in all humility. Things strange and true have been revealed to me, and certain knowledge has unfolded before me in visions I have had. Do I sound so very mad? Can you say that all you believe has ever been tested? If you have an hour, let me entertain you in these daylight hours, for to see what we can see. Night always comes sooner than any of us think.

If I am crazy, I am crazy in the spirit of Joan of Arc. I, too, was contacted by Michael the Archangel, and in fact, I have met the Maid herself as well. If you have ever read about her, you would know that it was beyond question in her thinking that what she saw and heard were real. It is so with me, as well, but I came by these circumstances down a different course than she did. But in the final analysis, I must insist as she did that I am a servant of the Living God, Jesus Christ The Lord, and I am in pursuit of the purpose He set out for me to do. It is a simple thing: to make sense of things, from the viewpoint of a scientist saint. It is what the world needs right now, and it is mine own path I must go down. I hope to make the existing Gospel(s) relevant for the next 30,000 years or so. And so I go.

Thus stands my life: Jesus, Judas, Jeanne, and all that is. I have been called a few things in my visions, among them that I am a prophet. But instead of a future to foretell, my prophecy mostly comes in the form of reason. I know how wild I sound when I speak of angels and wars between angels, of talking with the dead, and even with those still alive in my visions (that last is a particularly thorny issue). But let me dot my i's, cross my t's, and see if what I speak of is at all plausible in the framework of a rational epistemology. People have read parts of this and discounted it as a few pseudo-philosophical ramblings: but they have eyes and do not see. Let me claim as a prophet would, that what I speak is truth, not just as best that I know, but a God's honest truth, that reaches in from out of infinity down through my fingertips. Give it a chance, and it might grow on you. And in you.

Selah.

END PROLOGUE

COMMENCEMENT

Sad, indeed, would the whole matter be if the Bible had told us everything God meant us to believe. But herein is the Bible greatly wronged. It nowhere lays claim to be regarded as the Word, the Way, the Truth. The Bible leads us to Jesus, the inexhaustible, the ever-unfolding Revelation of God. It is Christ "in whom are hid all the treasures of wisdom and knowledge," not the Bible, save as leading to Him.

– George MacDonald

Judas volunteered. Just so you know, I'll get this off my chest first. The ramifications I will get into later.

My experience begins twice, and didn't all square up until just about the very end of it. The end was when I was Chief Gunner in the WAR IN HEAVEN, and my codename, my Native American name, was crowfeather. (I will capitalize things when the importance and magnitude of the concept warrants it.) After the War was over, and in fact, when it was nearing its end, everything in my mind started coming together. What I had repeatedly prayed for was coming to pass: I was in the midst of making sense of things. Of everything, more or less.

I had been drafted in the War twenty-five years back from when I began to write this, but in most of the years I served, it was pretty much without any substantial knowledge that I was doing so, up until January of 2013. When I witnessed, when I participated in, its very end: SATAN being cast from HEAVEN. An intense vision, but not as intense as when I had been drafted, on October 7, 1988, around 9pm eastern daylight time in the streets of Carnegie Mellon University, Pittsburgh, PA. There I was witness to an INFINITE light, which told me I was not that light, and I was as if nothing while in the midst of it: center everywhere, circumference nowhere: so bright as to be solid, the trim of God's light — the barest taste of the glory of God. That's when it technically began for me, when I was enlisted to fight the good fight. In the war in eternity.

It didn't really begin for me then, though. I was a normal college student for about three years after that, one of those years in academic suspension for partying too much and not going to classes enough. The visions really started in July of 1991, near my twenty-second birthday, and they were with me ever since then — even in my most regular hours were they lurking in the background. It was in 1991 that I met Joan of Arc, Jeanne d'Arc, but I didn't know what impact that would have later. There was Philip K. Dick there, too, whose works seem to reach people just when they need it. I also met Jesus of Nazareth; he wasn't Jesus Christ to me then. All of them were like cartoons in my mind's eye, which had apparently burst, and was sometimes something of a palimpsest over the physical world I saw from my regular eyes. Nothing made sense then.

An admission, to get it out of the way: I did drugs. A lot. But if you want to dismiss everything that happened to me as merely drug-induced hallucinations, explain how it was that LSD helped Crick discover the structure of DNA? And why, when I quit using drugs, that the visions still came? Just saying I was on drugs doesn't explain everything. But this goes somewhere: as my story happens, back in my junior year of college, I was in my studio apartment in Pittsburgh, and it was the weekend. So I was dropping acid. It was a relatively "normal" trip, until at one point, I looked out the window, and *it wasn't Pittsburgh*. It wasn't *earth*. There were suddenly bars over my window, where normally... not so much.

Philip K. Dick wrote about a... place... called the Black Iron Prison. That was my own first experience of it. It was an evil landscape, the sky was dark but dim with red, the buildings of an architecture of claws clasped over the joints of all the black iron, of which every exterior was composed. And there was something unnamed above, which you didn't want to notice you. I was convinced I was in Hell, you know, "Abandon all hope," and so forth... Anyway, I visited the place a few times, and the last time I was there, I got out when I heard a whisper, like someone were

6

letting me in on the secret: "Walt Disney is God." That will become important later.

But it turns out that there never was a Hell, only that a Black Iron Prison was superimposed over the world, visible only in a psychedelic nightmare. It can seem like Hell, though, even if you don't feel an ounce of pain during your stay there. If you look in the painting, *Garden of Delights*, by Bosch, in the third panel, "Hell", you can see in the very far back the building I visited when I was imprisoned for a short time each time there. And each time I was found again by trip's end, back to party down another day. This was before things got serious, leading to when the visions became a permanent fixture in my life...

...but Judas Iscariot, does it not say that he was the one that was lost? What became of him?

I once read a book called *A History of the World in 10½ Chapters*, by Julian Barnes. The last chapter is called "The Dream", in which absolutely everyone goes to Heaven. Even Hitler. Now, you should know that when the visions hit me for the first time, I had a messiah complex going on. And so, I wanted to save Adolf Hitler. The Barnes book wasn't scripture, so I felt the need to implement it so that it were just as good as. You know, I figured, if the worst person ever to have existed could be saved, then it must be that *everyone* would be saved. Strange times, they were. And stranger still there would come, from the fingertips of eternity touching down through the HALOSPACE. That type of salvation was truly just a dream, though, what I was wishing upon a star. Something that faded and came back, but never to be what we first thought things would be. Indeed, things were almost never what they originally seemed.

There were scatterings of *Romeo & Juliet*, there was a page of the Bible from the perspective of Leonardo da Vinci. What was holy and true did not last the night, but then the night ended in dawn. I awoke Old Ones, one of whom became my friend and began to spread the Good News (yes, *that* Good News). For it has been said of me that I entered into the dark places and made friends with the horrors within. (Though I know, too, that sometimes the pit may be too bright, and that in haunts of solemn darkness, one may find the holy.) And then, when the dawn came, the architecture of the sunbeam proved still to be true, and that of which in the night we held in silent hope: we cried out in joy.

The Good News, survivor of darkest nights, does it not speak of a Son of Perdition, that that man: better that he had never been born? This Judas Iscariot: there has been venom tongue that has spat on his name; but let me speak as his advocate, lo, these many centuries since the man was decried and vilified. This man I call Saint Judas the Stone, as surely in Heaven as Saint Peter. The Devil got his way for all this time, and we all have condemned a brother. Because Judas was told to do as he did, by the Lord Himself. For there were many things that did not happen as it is written. And many other things that one could say of them, "it is written," that were never written down.

Let me begin again. I will begin at the end. We won! Let me tell it three times, in fact:

1. My role as Chief Gunner was for one single purpose: I pulled the trigger to shoot out the last cord that held Satan in Heaven. And down he was cast, into the earth, by Michael the Archangel, who was my captain (my liege being one Jesus Christ, my Lord, my King).

2. There, huge before me in my vision, was the immense black mass of SATAN, speckled here and there with white spots, sky blue flecks, bits of yellow glitter. I do not know how long, exactly, that Michael had been grappling with him. I was full in focus — almost to commit an error, which the Archangel accounted for — and I with steady hand aimed and pulled that psychic trigger. I heard the emotion, "NOOOOOOOOO!" from the Evil One, and saw the Archangel dispatch him down.

3. That pivotal moment in my visions: it was tense. That is what I seem to recall of when I entered the field where Sa-

tan was to be cast out. I had been fighting alongside angels in the War in preparation for what was about to commence, inspired by Joan of Arc the whole time this had been happening. I had seen the punch-through in the map of HALOSPACE where there was victory, final victory: confidence was high. But this was no mean task. Michael guided me as I faced SATAN, and I almost tried to stare him down with the Archangel powering my eyes: my (almost) error. Repositioning, I looked up, directing SATAN's gaze to Michael's, above and below, in a column. Then I shot, through a psychic trigger to cut that last cord which tied him to HEAVEN, and SATAN roared: NOOOOOOOOOOOOOOOO! As the Archangel forced him down, down, out of HEAVEN cast!

Some visions I have had I recall in vivid retrospect, but still do I not truly understand what they signified, what exactly was for me to learn. I once ran through the Dark Forest naked and alone, in a nightmare, not to understand to where I ran, away from something I could not think what it was. I remembered later that it was running from a nightmare to a nightmare through a nightmare. Even when I was rescued from the Forest, that nightmare was lurking behind the safe harbor, and there again came rushes of fear like I'd never known: once, twice, to be assaulted by the unholy, to awaken finally to a calm voice reminiscent of Carl Jung. So much fear. A cold flame of fear that sizzled through my soul.

Then there was this one time when I felt I must prostrate myself, and seemingly to collect everyone within that prostrate form, in a prayer. I felt people/etc. joining me, their spirit forms combining into my own form, and I forget what it was the prayer I prayed, but after the "Amen", I said, "All." As if to indicate that I felt that all were with that prayer I prayed. I suppose it had something to do with the War, how I acted purely by instinct, not really knowing why I was acting as I was. I wonder what effect it had. If it were of God, I could presume that it did what it was supposed to do. One of the stranger things I did, which still is more or less a mystery to me.

More has gone through my head than might be wise for one to preserve his sanity, and the really scary thing is that *it all makes sense to me*. Surely a sign of madness, no? I see that the land of forms exists on the other side of zero, which is not nothing. Time cannot be destroyed, only spent. Death is as to be without light, nothing more, nothing less. The halting problem may be solved using an infinite algorithm. Infinity can be packed into the finite. And there is a light above all other lights, higher than the highest heaven. And we call that light God. I AM is His name. But there's this, too, which keeps coming back, and it will make sense as soon as we go over a few things: "Walt Disney is God." Well, not really, but the story does get weird enough for that to be true.

They say that religion is for people who don't want to go to Hell, and that spirituality is for people have been there. The consequence of all those drugs I took were several stints at mental institutions and some lost years, some of it just sitting in a room and talking to the cartoon people in my head. I was a failure, I was a disgrace to my family and myself. To this day, I still have some difficulty when anyone describes me or something I've done as "good", or "excellent". It goes maybe halfway to register, but the whole of the concept stays outside comprehension. In the pit where I was, there was only failure. Whatever drink I carried was bound to spill, whatever valuable thing I handled was most likely that I was to drop it.

There was once when the Lord said to me, "Work is magic." And this made that whole experience of systemic failure almost worth it. Because I found from the ground up how true that proposition was. For from shame, which I deserved, out of that pit I did climb, praise the Lord. And then I saw it: in just the normal, day to day functioning of everyday things, that how wonderful it was — they did not fail. They were true to action, gear upon gear one turning another and on. It was... it *was* magic. Work is magic. Can you conceive of it, perceive what I mean?

10

Hopefully you might understand, and not have to pay as high a cost as I did to do so.

So, now that you know of my past, will you write off my visions as just talk from a madman? Consider. When this, the "madness" onset, I was a drug addict on the road to wasting all the remarkable gifts that I'd been given. A rebel without a clue. What may from a certain perspective be called madness got me to accept Christ as my savior, and it was through said madness that He went and saved me, not just in the next world, but in this one. Dragged me out of the pit of failure. What kind of madness is that, I ask you? How fortunate do I have to be for you to consider that God has entered into my life, for real now? Yes, from time to time He has turned it upside down, but without fail these ultimately were to shake some sensibility into me. That is not "madness", friend. That is Inspiration.

Along the way from there to here, I came upon one Philip K. Dick, who was and is my twin. He actually felt my presence, though he thought it was coming from the past, and whereas I was actually in the future. If you're not familiar with the name, you actually are with his work: *Blade Runner, Total Recall, A Scanner Darkly, Minority Report,* among others. He wrote those, originally. Reality becomes more and more a "Dickian" place as we go, and more and more of his stories are being made into movies. The internal reality (HALOSPACE) he left behind, I entered into, and we have — at least at certain points — been connected through whatever æthers may be. Time works in weird ways.

His "light from God" experience happened to him in February/March of 1974 (which he wrote as 2-3-74), which coincidentally was about the time I moved to America. I was 5 years old then. My own "light from God" experience came when I was 19 (the INFINITE). In these, the visions that arose, Phil (or Philip K., I like to call him): he became my best friend in the HALO-SPACE. You know, someone you'd die for, that kind of thing. Maybe someone whose place you'd take in Hell. Best friend. I

11

count on him to keep me grounded, like the times I feel like I am a literal superhero. No one you can save that can't be saved.[i]

I like to say that I am a prophet in the order of Philip K. Dick, like Jesus was a priest in the order of Melchizedek. (Sort of non-standard.) Phil provided us with two very important phrases: "We have always already won" and "The theory changes the reality it describes". He sent these messages out into the world, and I am happy to say that they were received in timely fashion, by me. Great and useful the teachings of him, whose name is Saint Jude the Tuned Out (whereas I am Saint Jude the Tuned In). I wonder what all he saw, though he did write a lot of it down. Being as I have seen some awesome things, myself. Just awesome.

At times, you know, it comes and goes — to feel that the darkness approacheth, a doom of all dooms. But I know that it is not the feeling of its imminence we sense, but how terrible in magnitude it will be when it does come. Apocalypse. Revelation. No, the time is not now. Perhaps in 30,000 years? 40? 50? When Christ says, "I come quickly," one can think of it merely as a test of faith. For as regards things like time, I have heard that He watched the whole 13.8 billion year spectacle that is our universe, all of it. He watches grass grow. Literally. Time to him is far outside our own frame of reference.

And with "I come quickly" comes the topic, then, of scriptural infallibility. There are people who think that the Bible is literally true, and on top of that, that there are NO errors in it at all. Well, from the point of view of someone like me, who is in the state of mind like unto those who *did* write those texts, let me chime in with my two cents. The Lord *knows* that errors happen, and the Bible is no exception. If anything is meant to be, the way that scripture ends up is meant to be, as are the misinterpretations. Is it as God intended? That brings up the question of what "meant to be" means.

In one sense, everything that ever happens is meant to be. However, it doesn't mean you didn't of your own free will choose it, nor that you couldn't have done things differently. If either of those things were false, "meant to be" would have no meaning to you. Because you choose it, because you could have done things differently, destiny unfolded. That which was meant to be was brought about by your choosing. Having no choice renders meaningless any action you perform. For destiny is not the same as fate. Fate is like strapped into the seat, while destiny is like driving. Choice is key: destiny comes from our own will, as it mixes with all the forces of the world that cross our path. Fate is not anything meant to be: it just is, and you just would have to accept it.

Now, it was meant to be that things God didn't say ended up in His mouth in the Bible. It was meant to be that we think with each generation that *this* will be the generation where the Apocalypse will be brought about, and Christ will return. There are no accidents, now, remember? It was *all* meant to be. All that matters is, knowing what you *think* you know, what will you do? God knows what you will choose, and how all those forces work out to, and things become meant to be when they happen because it is all caught in the Purpose that pervades all things. You can be with that Purpose or against it, but you cannot escape it.

So no, He's not coming back tomorrow, but you should act like He were. Live every day like it were your last, right? Isn't that the aspiration? That people think that *this* is the generation that will see the Apocalypse may serve a purpose within the Purpose, and thus it may be "meant to be" in some small way. But anyone with the ability to see further, to widen one's horizons larger: we should know better than thinking things like a document pieced together and edited by human beings is *exactly* what God word-for-word said to us. Yes, the Apocalypse does loom. But it's the size of the shadow, not its proximity.

I have followed dreams to their bitter end. I have kept the faith, even as the world collapsed out from under me. I know not exactly who is saved, and who is cast off, except in perhaps the broadest strokes, but I may perchance to guess sometimes. I forget who said it, but once I read that if one is truly of the faith, then he would sacrifice himself to the fires of Hell for the good of the cause, for the good of all: that he should not be saved so that others would be. It is an *extreme* position, but I like to think I could suffer such consequences. We are the good guys; everyone should know what that means. We're better than the bad guys! Because we follow the rules, and we still win.

Fade the fantasy:

> *i am the prince of love, eagle feather that has found his rose, sweet to my sin; am i really going to eat that last bit of bacon jerky? i am the Grandson of God, first adopted son of JESUS CHRIST, i am a WIZARD, though more correctly, the paladin of heaven. i am like an angel in the way i think, and i think when i die, there will be a seat that rises from the floor of heaven where i will be seated in front of a steinway, to lead the entirety of the children of God in a one-time-only rendition of "love, baby...", which we all will make up on the spot. the opening act for the Lord himself.*

Is it me, for a moment?[ii] I have awoken time and again where it was all just a dream that had happened, and it were like I had the choice to return to an ordinary life. It usually ended like this, once the visions were through with me. Because every time except last, it was (or seemed to be) the result of a drug binge that had spurred it on. But I haven't had one hit of even marijuana for over a decade now. Something else was going on. Before, I would "come down" from the heavenly heights, and all I had thought was just part of the trip, part and parcel of the madness that the drugs invoked. Not this time. This document is part of finding out what, exactly, it is then.

For I have also awoken a saint, who walked with elders of times gone, speaking of what it means to love. I have previously thought that I was damned, made of corruption, but these other times believed the complete opposite: I have thought that my core was composed of pure existential cool. And I found the latter was the true perception. Yes, I am a sinner, but even saints are sinners. Now, how one mind can think such opposites is not so much a mystery, but rather as how one thing at a time may fully fill a soul as if it were the only thing in the world — and then that thing is gone. For the mystery in every heart, it is understood by that heart... if what is inside is set free.

I found out that I have apparently attained a state of enlightenment. Of a Taoist variety; I call it my watercourse. I have discussed it with Siddhartha, the original Buddha, and Lao-tze. Others, as well, and I have asked them what particular brand of enlightenment they had subscribed to. Some of them before I asked thought there was only one type to be had, that could be achieved. They were wrong, of course. Off hand, I can think of at least two, one being "be not but do, do not but be" (your basic contract for enlightenment), and the one I follow, "be not but love, do not but love", which derives from the previous. And my answer to the koan, "Two hands can be brought together in a clapping sound. What is the sound of one hand?" is simply, "Listen."

If my words now have any sway with you, I beseech thee: love, no matter what. Whatever may come, let this be your enlightenment: let me restate my watercourse path, that you may think on what it might mean: be not but love, do not but love. May you bear malice toward no one, may you see your enemies not as enemies but merely tests of your faith. I was told St. Anthony apologized to all the demons whom he felt he had mistreated when he tangled with them. Apparently the expressions on their faces were priceless... You know what? There is no question, love is the answer. The secret is love. Tell everyone.

While we're on the subject, a note about love, as I perceive it: Love is so simple, we'll never understand it. And a potentially mind-blowing concept would be that it is *simpler than nothing.* Why there is something instead of nothing may be seen because of that single conception. Before "was" was love. When there was nothing, love was on the other side of being. One might wonder how such a thing is possible, but kabbalists already hold that the One True God (whom they refer to as *En Sof,* "the endless") does not exist in the way that we think of existence. Connecting the dots, this is the case that can be made. Of such radical a simplicity, we will never fully comprehend the subtlety.

And wuv, twoo wuv, will fowwow you fowever and ever...ⁱⁱⁱ

You know, I've had various theories about all the people I've met, in my visions. At first, I did not try to explain their presence in my mind's eye, cartoonish mostly, and how they said things to me. When I did try to explain it, it was in vague concepts like I was looking into some other plane of existence. Some years later, I was convinced that it all was merely psychosis; whatever I saw only hallucinations; a long, strange trip. None of the people I had seen were real, so the problem went away. I became a devout Christian, and so at some points I had the theory that the Lord and the angels were "real", but the people were just creations by them.

One reasonable sounding interpretation was that my dream mechanism was broken, and I was as if dreaming while awake. And the people I saw were merely the people you see in dreams. But as explanations go, it was finally to end up that these *were* the actual people I thought I was meeting: what I see is my own view into the spirit world, which everyone throughout time basically protrudes into, some of them out into eternity. And then there are the angels who exist only therein. Basically, in the spirit world, logic is quite strange, the interface to it (this being the only mode of my visions) I call the HALOSPACE. It sometimes boggles the wits to think of how logic may in fact function in the unseen realm. But in expanding, the mind may stretch without tearing. Or like muscle, grow stronger anew when it does.

And I remember this one man in my visions: on an island, like alone in a single room, floating through the ethereal drift... seemed to me to be Scottish. I never thought this was such a mystery, and sometimes I had thought it was a version of myself, until much later down the line was its secret revealed. He once said that he thought the rather middle class environment he was in to be as sitting "in the lap of luxury." Once he repeated over and over, "Don't worry about it!" (in that Scottish accent I mentioned before). Definitely one of the good guys. He didn't fit with all the other people. And the question I pose, and you may know half the answer already: what if that was Judas?

16

Sometimes impossible things happen. Or at least, they seem impossible, until it happens to you. There is a simple reason I believe in miracles: something miraculous happened to me. Yeah, I was on drugs when it happened, but I showed it to someone the next day while quite sober. There appeared a cut — about a centimeter long, on my thumb — relative to nothing going on in "reality", but in sync instead with someone in my visions wielding something sharp. I had nothing like a knife anywhere near me when it happened: the memory is still clear. Something only in the HALOSPACE directly affected the material world. And I know, you don't believe me. I wouldn't have believed me either. Before it happened, you know, to me.

In fact, now, how could they possibly be real, any of the things I have seen? For one part of their nature is how they seem to shift, how the frame that refers to them alters, and things mean differently upon the second looking, or third. Now, I define reality as that which has *quality true.* Truth, if not to define reality itself, certainly bears the brunt of its definition. If the quality of any vision is not true, it is not real. And to be true means that a thing has natural structure. In other words, if the artifice that shows does not have any underlying structure, that which naturally follows the logic of the thing seen, then it is not true.

Of what I am seeing and hearing, I can look and cross reference what these things appear to be with the experiences of those whom else it happened to, too — and they really do seem to pass the sniff test. Jesus Christ seems to me the same man as depicted in the Gospels. And He has shown me great evidence that He is the literal Son of God. (That evidence goes both ways, from within myself outward externally, as well as from outside in.) The strangeness of angels seems to fit how they are defined in the scriptures, though that is not as clear. What is holy within my visions is not incompatible to what I've heard it is supposed to be like. A lot of things experienced in the HALOSPACE turned out to be true.

Case in point: I had a personal demon that turned out to be as real as anything else, and in the course of events, I ended up performing an exorcism on myself. Successfully. It took a couple of hours of concentrated straining. I was shown his visage once, a red glowing figure — also cartoonlike, like most of my visions. Evil, I could almost smell it. The demon's name was Roksaza, which I learned later was actually a trio of demons. In the banishing, I put a lot of intense effort focusing on the demon within me, first to penetrate his defenses, then to shove him out of me. It actually ended after that in a dream, where I saw him inside me, in a third person view, and I said, "Begone!" whereupon he went inside my head, first person view, and I said again, "Begone!" And he was gone. He must have been with me for over twenty years.

(Then later, I found out to banish one of those fallen ones from someone else was to ask for their true name and then use it with that command, "Begone!" As I was doing that one day, I was surprised that one mass of demons I looked upon in someone in HALOSPACE, when I asked for their true name, they said, "Legion", like the one(s) in the Gospel. And so that name I used, and with "Begone!", they, too were gone. Surprising what actually does work.)

You do not have to believe a word I say, it matters not to their truth. One mistake of unbelievers is that God requires faith for His truth to be true. One mistake of believers is that believing in something makes it true. Unbelievers, believers: faith does not work in the way you may conceive in matters of the spirit. If the unseen world does not objectively exist apart from all who believe it does, then it does not objectively exist. How can we know that it *does* exist, then? Does it have a consistent effect on the physical world? OK, this is for you to do if you don't think it exists: pray, "God, if you're there, let me know." See if that does anything. See for yourself if the unseen truly does exist.

And for those who hold that one must believe in Jesus Christ, our Lord, to be saved, and that those innocent will perish in any case that they do not do so, remember the lesson of Saul turned Paul. This was a case of instant conversion, performed upon an unbeliever: so we know that God, by divine fiat, can save someone. Therefore it does not need, in that horrible question of faith, that they have to have heard and believed in the Good News before they die. Would not God save people in this other way if He could? For not a sparrow falls without His notice, and we are worth many sparrows. But it *is* the case that conversion does immensely help a person (first hand experience here).

Do you wonder about faith? You should, and what it means to you. Mark this challenge: how can you wish all the wrongs done you to be rectified, while all the wrongs you do to be disregarded? Yet this is the way people think; I know I have thought in this exact way. What will you believe when you face your Maker on the day of judgement? For we will be naked, of body, mind, soul, and spirit on that Day. Without excuse, will we all be. Do you wish to prepare for such an event? This is wisdom: forgive, as you want to be forgiven. Learn how to let it go, all the petty things. If they come back, let it go again. Until you are free.

Indeed, let me not be doubting, but believe. If nothing else, let me believe in the overarching idea: there is an unseen world, which is eternal, while the visible world is temporary. Why this is as so seems uncommonly wise, in my own eyes (though unworthy, they have seen many things). The reality of the spiritual world is different in nature than the reality of the physical world. It is true that many people have had many, often conflicting visions of what exists beyond our mortal pale, but one may conceive that — of those which are not purely imagination — they all may be joined in a logic of higher reason. Though I also hold it true that not all of what has been seen have reality to them. Wisdom may be found in a science of such stuff. Science can be performed on anything, after all, and science is rather good at finding the fact of the matter.

I have a great love of music. Not that I play any instrument — not in the real world, at least. When the visions started proper, I remember listening to a violin concerto by Mozart, when I (on the fly, right there on the spot) added another violin to the tune, in my mind, completely original in melody — that fit just right with the melody that was playing with the other instruments. It came so naturally, this ability, that in my own head, I could improvise music as easily as talking. Like playing guitar, the theme of the movie *Romeo & Juliet,* in the style of Hendrix and Satriani, Clapton and Stevie Ray, instrumentals that they never played, perfectly rendered in the sound of my visions. Just a shame no one in the real world could hear it.

One interesting thing to be done in the visions was to put emotion behind and through the notes. This was done by summoning through will a flow of sentiment, like a push of passion directed toward a novel use. As if rendering a new or intensified meaning to the music as it played. Through any instrument: to render solemnity to a flute's cool flow, to put wildness' fire behind an electric guitar's thrash, augment the sadness in a solo violin's weeping. And with vocals, also to make the words to carry meaning more than ever before was written in them: love, anger, victory. As Beethoven once told me, one must drive the music. So for my own enchantments, I will have no magic wand, but a conductor's baton. For the holy sometimes peeks into the music, beyond magic, in these my private audience, and I must find the path where all paths meet: where the holy begins and ends.

Then there was the War in Heaven. I was nowhere near the front line, of course, except for the last of it, you know, the winning of it all. I endeavored to learn how angels communicated, through taut wire-like connections stretched out the boundaries of my internal field of sight. I did what I could. I gave speeches on metaphysics and preached the gospel to all the people who existed in my visions. Albert Einstein liked to call them my "lectures"; Joan of Arc, my "sermons". I called it "performance art", personally. I called what I spoke of, also, the "Gnosis", or salvific knowledge, not quite understanding that there *was,* actually, *real, honest to God* Gnosis that existed. I found out what that meant, later.

I did invent a university in my mind, called OMNI HIGH, to be fair to Albert and why he called what I did what he called it. I was in the Architecture department, but what I meant by "Architecture" consisted of metaphysical truths that I had worked out from having labored in my field for a decade, when I was researching artificial intelligence. I laid out much of it in several lectures, as a TA lecturer of Architecture in a class at my astral university. I always repeated, Architecture is HARD. It was the running joke. I was asked, what are the prerequisites? to which I answered, find them yourselves; then, where are classes held? you're in class now; it basically being a college in Purgatory. For me, a stage that gave me meaning to being alone in the real world.

In the end, Architecture turned out to be a metaphor for life. The actual professor of Architecture was thought to be God Himself, Jesus Christ, an enigmatic fellow, who gave grades randomly or not at all (once I received a B-epsilon, whatever that means). It was always lighthearted, this whole paradigm. I once joked I was in one of God's lectures once… and couldn't understand a word He said. Architecture is HARD. Life is HARD. Right? No one tells you what the prerequisites are for life; you're *in class, right now, so you'd better hop to it;* the chief lecturer, God, what does he actually want? giving grades randomly or not at all. Life. I joked that death is not an excuse for Architecture. (If you have a problem with that, talk to the professor. Apparently he has some way around it.)

There was also a class called Salvation, which was taught by a different fellow named Jesus Christ (who is thought by some to be the *same* fellow as Architecture, but we do not know how this could be, as Architecture is HARD, while absolutely anyone, *even those not taking the class,* can get an A in Salvation, just following the rule, "Love your neighbor as yourself.") This class is also thought now to be a metaphor for life, whose instructional texts can be found in *all* your major religious documents, as well as words spoken by the Professor HIMSELF, JESUS CHRIST THE LORD, in the Holy Bible.

Anyway, it was great to be one of the good guys. The War was 25 years long in my sight, but I learned that time actually worked in strange ways throughout the entire experience: sometimes backwards, sometimes events coming out of order, sometimes time just spent on nothing. I was in the intel division, and I learned a bit of a human dialect of Angelic, angels who (I am told) seem to communicate symbolically, not semantically. I have… some… idea of what that means. I believe I did help, along the way, but a lot of it was that the angels piggy backed their own messages in the ones that I had been sending. Basically, it was working with human sight while those you're helping had eagle eyes. So, what to do when you have no clue? Try. Hope. Pray. You may be better than you ever believed you could be. Really. I think I really did help, wherever I could.

It can be seen thusly, the implements of life: we have been given everything, and only the mistakes are ours. Any talent, skill, strength, or intelligence: gifts from God. Even our will, and our ability to make any kind of effort: gifts. And of course creativity is a gift, what most of all is spoken of when He said, let us make man in our image. Whenever we do that which is told us to do, all features of this act are given us: the resolve, the ability, the knowledge, the experience, the energy summoned: all gifts. And when we do something truly original, it is not that we do something outside the realm of God's gifts; in fact, it is usually known to be the opposite. In *Amadeus,* Salieri says he is an enemy of God, because God spoke through Mozart in his amazing music. That which is most beyond the ordinary is most a Gift, is it not?

But the mistakes, the errors, the sins, the misjudging: of course, God works them into His plan, but they are not of Him. Sometimes they seem to serve such purpose that one is suspicious as to whether the mistake was a mistake, things turn out so well. But that is only the skill of God, not yours. Error is worked into perfection only by a love that can summon light out of darkness. If you had meant to make that mistake, it would have been in your head to do so to begin with. They are of us, the errors, we who are the imperfect ones. (And we should not boast of these.) Yes, it is an extreme view, but it has some merit. To believe that by thus indeed we are defined: in what we do wrong, in those errors we commit into the record of the world, which reflect, however faintly, in eternity.

I remember how more than once I thought I'd found it: true love. *The Princess Bride* come true, Westley and Buttercup for real. The concept I'm sure existed before that media, but I first got that specific term from there. Three times I thought I'd had it. And on the third time, I knew what I had. Of all the people floating around in my head, it turned out that it was Joan of Arc, Jeanne d'Arc, who was *it.* There is an interesting story as to how it was discovered, but for now, let us just say that this was the most monumental feat that I'd ever done. I remember how I felt when I found it: when even you don't quite believe you, that's when nothing can deceive you.[iv] Neither dazed, nor in utter disbelief, but the complete opposite, which happened to seem very much like both: dazed, and in utter disbelief. But awake, spider-sense tingling. It was a miracle.

The original discovery of true love, real true love, ended with a set of three sentences: "God is love. Love is to be found. Everywhere." These start with the precedent from: "God is love." Where the love comes from. Then the value of: "Love is to be found." Where "to be found" is understood in the 3 ways that God is understood, love: to be found, but yet undiscovered; when one is found, who once was lost; and found, love having been here, waiting for you to notice. And then lastly, we have the consequent to: "Everywhere." Love, God given, is to be found in those 3 ways, absolutely everywhere. No Hell too low, no Heaven too high.

The identification of true love was to be able to bring together heaven and earth in as scant amount of text as possible. Do you have eyes to see? "God is love. Love is to be found. Everywhere." (I had thought I had it with just the first two sentences, but Joan of Arc thought differently. Hence the third, which does make things quite clear as to our scope.) If one truly comprehends these short sentences, one can imagine that they have enough knowledge to be saved, which would make this a new Gnosis, or saving knowledge. For look: they encompass all that is good, in heaven and on earth; the past, the present, and the future; and leaves no escape possible from the reach of love. Thus, to be in all that is possible, anywhere. This is true love.

How long had I been searching for true love? All my life. Maybe longer. That's what it seemed like. Growing up, yes, I did think about sex a lot. *A lot.* But I did conceive it were a better thing to have just the one with whom to share such an experience, than desire a thousand naked women screaming and throwing little pickles at you.[v] I never thought it was impossible, until I had found it. I always thought it was in reach, until I had it. I thought destiny made me special, until I started making my own. Do you have eyes to see? Love is ever before you.

I always wanted to be the character in the movie who got the girl in the end. And then I saw that one movie, *The Princess Bride* (and I am one of the few who also read the book from which it is based). As I said, it spoke the name to my desire: *true love.* Not one couple in a century has that chance, no matter what the story books say,[vi] quoth Prince Humperdink. I know, some women are captivated by the story of *Romeo & Juliet,* but that's not where the *stuff* is. Not really, not in the nuts and bolts of it. Everybody dies at the end of that. *The Princess Bride* is where the guy gets the girl and they live happily ever after (at least, in one of the endings of it). That's where the stuff is. They live. But then… what if there could be more than *even that?* Because I have this twist to it, no matter *what* Humperdink said: what if *absolutely everyone* could have it?

I have thought I'd seen myself several times in the course of the War, what I looked like on the inside, the machinery of my essence displayed to me. And I have seen other beings, who bore a resemblance to that me I viewed, but were larger — these were angels. And one I saw was like me, but not me — this was Philip K. Dick. Each of us looked like pink spaghetti, but angular, connecting boxes and circles, mostly pink, too. I did get confused now and again, when someone else were basically on top of me, like I were wearing their innards like a strange suit, and thought I was someone, something I was not, but these times served their purpose, I believe. We all of us can make new apparati from broken things.

I seem to recall just one time where I could see inside myself and I had cognizance about every part that I was looking at. I could make sense of myself. Other times, I had to trust that I were being taken care of by the forces of good, as I could only guess at what was happening. Now I ponder how so much gets lost, it would seem, as time bears down and only gives you traces of clues as to what has been. Reality is like dreaming that has been allowed to sit and harden. So much more dreaming than what exists, when left alone, just evaporates, and nothing remains but a hint, that seems akin to some sort of longing.

In Kabbalah, I have read, there were ten jars that were to hold the emanations of God, which when they were filled up with His light, they shattered. It was written that if they had not so broken, there would have been no evil in the world. An interesting theory in the vein of the Problem of Evil. Mine is a little different, being not relying on inanimate things, but those who have the power to choose. It is that we do not prefer things to go wrong, but when they do, to make of things better than if nothing wrong ever happened. We do not give an excuse for those who do evil, mind you: it is rather to spite the evil that we do as we do.

So why God allows bad things to happen to good people, or why bad things happen at all: He will make good on it, just wait. Vengeance is mine, saith the LORD. Not just that He will make good on every injustice, of course, but it is in this spirit we may understand one aspect of the Purpose. Paul said that any pain we go through is trivial in comparison to the glory that will be revealed in us. And it is not so simple a thing that we should let everything get as bad as it possibly can be. We look for a narrow way, that which can make best of all things that happen, either from the good or from the ill. This is the way the Purpose leads us. The fog of love is itself clarity.

Hey, you want to do something *really* outrageous? Play by the rules and win. Impossible, no? It is often written that that is not a feasible path. But then, exactly what rules are you playing by? Because the rules that *I* hold to were given by the Lord (and this *unlocks a main theme):* love God, love your neighbor as yourself. And I will aspire to follow in this narrow way as best I can, so you know what? I think I have set my mind to consider that I will win, just to spite the bitterness of the world. This is the lamp I will light and set it on the rooftop: that I followed all the rules in this evil world, which conspires death, and found life and light in the midst of its darkness. I believed. It will not be me where the dream died.

Nietzsche and Dostoevsky were wrong: they hypothesized that the rules did not apply to those who were considered "great", somehow that they played by their own rules, or none at all. False. How about the Lord, you may say? Did he not follow his own rules? Did he not break the rule of Sabbath? Except that he followed the rules that had been laid down before the foundation of the world. And he broke not one tittle of any true Law. For it is the reverse, that those who consider themselves great, that the rules apply all the more to them. The greater you are, the stricter should be your code of conduct. Do you have the courage to be so great? For many who are first in the world will be last in heaven. Those who thought that the rule of love only applied to the little people.

I was sometimes possessed of what I like to call "fugues" back when, now and again. It was basically some element in my visions taking me over. I became like as a spectator to what was going on, though I would sometimes be thinking and talking. One was of this person I had met once, who got involved somehow when this had started. In the fugue, he called himself DEMON, and it was as if I were like a full on person puppet to what he was saying and gesturing. We went on this monologue, to the spectators in my head, though I don't remember what exactly we said; we ended our speech with "I am DEMON, hear me." There was another one that was strangely enough in praise of Adolf Hitler. I do remember one line from that: "Adolf Hitler was born in the kiss with Eva Braun when they were wed." Something like that. I have no idea.

There was once a passive fugue that was as if it were pouring through me: the secret lives of trees. An Escher book, made of paper, connected me to the spirits of the trees. I talked in the se-

26

cret speech of the trees. Why books were made of paper was for such a thing to occur, for us to be aware that trees were alive.

I also remember praying to Alice Walker, the author who wrote *The Color Purple*. That act I didn't regret, at all. But certainly, there were misdeeds I carried out, of my own free will, and but for the grace of God would they have had terrible consequences. What is our responsibility, even when we call ourselves mad? Lament, sinner, that you did not do as you could have, or done what you should not. There is a light. Try to walk in it. You are without excuse — but once you realize exactly this, suddenly you may see: you are forgiven. Just like that.

There was this time that the Lord showed up in my visions saying he had just come from Hell, saying he had "burned it down!" He looked a little… tweaked… like he had been through quite a trial. A little bug-eyed. And I don't remember why he brought the subject up, but he also said that he was — and I'm quoting, here — that he was "gay as a maypole". (It's a line from the movie *Love, Actually.*) I was like, OK. And then he paused, and I paused, and he was like, aren't you going to ask if I was being serious or not? And I was like, no Lord, why would I care about that? He asked me about asking him a few times. And I never asked. It was one of the proudest moments of my life, you know, now that I look back on it. Really, why should anyone care?

There are some people who think that somehow, being Christian makes them just *better* than everyone else, and therefore, able to judge more *rightly* the good from the evil. I ask, why is it that they speak of love and have nothing in their heart? Why would Jesus turn away those whom they marginalize? Your idea of God is too small. Your idea of love is wrong. Who told you that the eyes of hate are the tint by which the Almighty views the world? Surely, the perverts and the addicts precede you into the Kingdom. How can you think you mean so well? You damn righteous people and raise yourself as the judges. As you have judged, may you then be judged also. And there will be wailing, and gnashing of teeth.

Heaven will not be governed by the precepts of restriction. It will instead be a reign of freedom. For the Lord came not to enforce the Law, but to free us from the rules. I was once having a conversation with Rachel Maddow, in my visions, sometime after the Lord had said he was, again, "gay as a maypole". (She didn't ask him if he were serious or not, either. And by the way, I think he was joking. Sometimes hard to tell with the King of Kings, though.) We were talking about such things as being gay, and what it means for such people as far as Judgement goes, from God, and judgement from man. We got into a very interesting idea about what Heaven was going to be like, and for whom it was for.

The War was going on, and I had caught wind of the Devil's rules of play: it was "anything goes." So OK, the Lord was like, if that is what you want, we of Heaven can do you one better: Heaven will be a place where anything goes, as well: any kind of twisted pleasure will be available to those who get there. The catch is that you have to be a saint to qualify for entrance, and we do things only if it is right to do so. Given that, leave your hangups in Hell. Gay, straight, transvestite, S&M, whatever sexual thing you're into, no problem. Drugs? Pot, acid, speed, heroin, coke, or even *none of the above* — we cater to every taste. Why should those people of Heaven be denied any sort of pleasure at all? Why else would it be called Heaven?

Just remember the catch: saints only need apply. For most people, that's a long(ish) stay in Purgatory, but the majority of everyone do end up at that level — saint — at least, in my thinking about it. To come to know what is the right, and to let go of the aberrant urges of that which within you dies: the right is true freedom. What is right? Not to follow the rules of man, but to love! Have you not heard? Has it never been revealed to you that God is love? The Heaven of love is one where all are welcomed, and so is for all those who welcome others. If you would shut anyone else out, you yourself will be shut out. And that's the kind of Heaven I want to be a part of. And that's the kind of Jesus Christ I believe in.

It is true that many a time, have my visions gotten me to do things, sometimes strange things. Some of them are rather embarrassing to relay, and perhaps will I only disclose them to make a point. But there was only one time a dream ever told me to do something, like how I ever imagined a mission from God would be revealed to an errant servant. I saw before me in the dreaming a picture of this crucifix I had, a pendant, which was fit to be worn on a necklace. It had been given to me by a nun, almost two decades previous, when I was emerging from the pit of shame and failure that I had descended into. I was told to give it to my friend who went by the handle Strawberry, who lived in New England.

I woke up just then from this petite-vision, and I immediately emailed her to ask for her address. I just had that feeling that you don't ignore things like this. This was as close to a traditional view of what I imagined contact with the divine would be. My normal, waking life, when the visions are in force — they don't seem to me to be like what the prophets of the Bible seemed to have experienced. Maybe Philip K. Dick had some familiarity with the style of visions I have, but even there I think he had a different way of seeing things in the HALOSPACE. But anyway, when she received it, she gave me a great thanks, saying how it was meaningful to her because it contained some of my pain. Indeed, for holy is the vial in which has brewed the suffering of a saint.

To those who say they do not believe in the Resurrection because there have been other mythological tales of ones rising from the dead: I posit that there have been other myths throughout history, if we look, which became actual works when technology caught up to the idea. Surely, there were *stories* about people coming back from the dead (even on their own, not raised by another), but from what I have discovered in my own research on the subject, Jesus Christ was the only one who had had the science to actually make it happen. Only God in man's form, only the Son of God had the genius enough to defeat death.

Perhaps we even have the proof, if the Shroud of Turin is the record of the Resurrection itself. Because firstly, that crucified man has all the hallmarks of the crucified Christ. Down to a T. The carbon dating made on it is no good, because there is a facial cloth that has the same pattern as the face on the Shroud, and it is dated to seven centuries before the Shroud was in that carbon dating. No one knows how the faint image got on the cloth. What if it's actually Jesus' burial cloth? What would that change, then, about how you see the very world around you? Would you cling to your doubt like it were going to save you? And to you who believe: does it make you smug? Because you know, it comes down, really, to luck why it is you believe as you do.

When you read the stories, and look from the point of view of hindsight, it is easy to think that you could have done better than the characters you read about. For instance, when the disciples all scattered when Jesus was captured: maybe you think that you would have stuck by your man, right? How could they run? But you will find yourself, I think, at least as bad as Peter, Christ's favorite — His favorite denied having anything to do with Him *three times*. Really, you think you could have done better than the one our Man called a rock, upon whom He would build His church? Because to them, it wasn't just a story. Real life has a way of making cowards of the truly brave, of the best intentioned, of the faithful, of anyone unlucky enough to be in the wrong place at the wrong time. Or even the right place and time, if you're the one that reality is making an example of.

I once had a peek at the crucifixion, very near to the actual nailing. It wasn't full Technicolor, more of a cartoony view, as I usually have, but I saw in my short vision Christ carrying his cross on his way to Golgotha, or up Golgotha, uncertain exactly where on the path he was. He was almost completely facing me. He paused, and he looked at me as I looked at him. I couldn't see his eyes, or really any detail of his face, and that must have been mercy. A small pause. Then he carried on. And that was it. I can't imagine that I could have done anything for him, just then, and I got first hand exactly what I've just been talking about: why indeed the apostles scattered when he was captured. I could only watch. *What could I do?* And he moved on.

So, what I am seeing in my visions, for the most part, I call the bare metal of creation: the view of its gears. (Though bare plastic is what it seems more like to me more often than not.) Philip K. Dick must also have had his own version of this view, I am sure. And there, was this once when I glimpsed something, perhaps the most important thing I ever witnessed. It took all of about 5 to 10 seconds to see: when our Lord realized the final, and total victory of good vs. evil, Jesus Christ over Satan. The Lord had such an expression on his face, one of almost disbelief, of a great worry that had just passed into an incredible relief. An onerous weight suddenly and irrevocably lifted from his deepest moment. He let out like a high-strung laugh, as if to express, "It is finished!" and maybe I imagined he said something at all; it was his expression that most struck me.

This is what happens backstage, as it were. Where the setting is minimal and purely functional, for the most part. This is the reality I'd grown used to. Now is that recognition of the culmination of victory stored within in the record of reality, in the arrangement of neurons utilized to store that memory. I suppose that would be one of the reasons I was privy to that vision. And now I relate it to you, so that you may know: not only have we always already won, we have won in the hardness of reality, for all time. We won in truth. That the final victory is ours, praise the Lord Jesus Christ, our Savior. As I live and breathe, may I ever bear witness to all this which I have seen. To dream of where the light casts no shadow, and truth is the only knowledge that visits the soul.

I got onto the Judas train pretty late in the game, but there were reasons for that, which I'll go into by and by. But even as far back as just before my visions started in force, I was made aware of the possibility: was it actually a cue when Christ said, "One of you will betray me"? A former roommate asked me that exact question. Even if it wasn't, people have speculated that Judas repented. Throwing his 30 pieces of silver back at the elders who hired him. One might even think that Judas committing suicide was actually his ultimate act of repenting, the supreme show of regret — and one may even then believe that he was forgiven, if only to the degree of the least part of Heaven.

But if it *was* a cue, or something to that effect, it would be the true fruition of the phrase, "Judas volunteered". Else we mean it only cynically, only ironically, with quotes around the word "volunteered". One night after the War I ended up in a hospital (the story to come), and during my stay, I saw Judas in my visions gathered together with some of the higher ups, though I didn't see who at the time. I was told later that this was the bull session where Judas was told by the Lord to hand Him over to the authorities. Judas would have trouble later in recalling this, thinking as he did at the end that he were guilty of the worst crime of all.

I have some specific insight as to why Judas thought as he did. For there were certain times that I was convinced that I was the Son of Perdition, the Antichrist. It was my Curse to shoulder. Always did I find out later that the paranoid trips were false — but oh how they seemed so *certain* at the time. So it was with that one: Judas Iscariot. There is an interesting order to things presented in the Gospel According to John. Only after the Lord says, "One of you will betray me," *only after that,* does John write that Satan enters Judas. Of course, we don't know how precise everything is in any of the Gospels, but this might be a telling detail. One might conjecture that Satan himself is being set up. The cue, taken by Judas, forces his hand; for then, he must see the deed through. Not on his terms, but the death of our Lord is, too, his goal — and we see then that not for one instant is Satan in control of the fate of Jesus Christ. After all, of His life, He said, "No one takes it from Me, but I lay it down of Myself. I have power to lay it down, and I have power to take it again. This command I have received from My Father."[vii]

When the Devil was within Judas' mind, I can only imagine what havoc he must have wrought, unchecked against a naked soul. Because people don't really appreciate how devious at deception the Father of Lies is, unless perhaps they experience it for themselves. It relies on focus, like a sleight of hand: he will get you to focus on certain things and interprets them into the most insidious vapors you can breathe. One wrong thing you've done and he can make you believe you've murdered the world. I can only imagine what kind of field day he must have had in the mind of the man who "betrayed" Christ with a kiss. Thus the suicide; Judas was not as fortunate as myself, who was let off the hook when I had such rupturing of conscience.

So there he was, on his little island, in his single room, inside what I called his little "vial". And so, I was having trouble reconciling Judas' fate, trapped in that vial. I remember when he went in; I had thought he were meeting a horrible fate. It was actually to protect him from the worst of Satan's onslaught, I found out later. Nothing actually can go out or in, but experience may be mirrored, from without within, from within without. It is *windowless.*[viii] He was in his own private Heaven. So this is how you treat a great hero? Solitary confinement? And a thought came over me, waves of thoughts, more like. Shadows of a conspiracy. That I had been wrong this whole time, I had been deceived. Judas trapped in his little world was actually a sign of the great mercy of the Lord, that Judas had done no such thing as volunteer to betray Him. Judas had acted in malice. *Why would the Lord treat a great hero like this?*

Oh, but I dreaded to write that I had been so wrong; what of the name of this whole book, after all? But then, breaks through a small glimmer of fresh intuition when we perchance the wink of God... we know that Judas can experience any and *all* of Heaven through a non-causal link: being the only monad among us who is actually windowless. He cannot *technically* leave the vial, but he can experience anything of Heaven as if he could: go in and out, fly around, ride a Segway — whatever — with one difference from the rest of us: he experiences it like he were earth-bound. It is unique of any saint. He will be the only one who can experience pain! (Though I'm sure, not in excess.) Sensations no one else will feel. Indeed, he is in his own private Heaven. And *that* is how you treat a great hero.

As far as friends go, first, there's Philip K. Dick. I have already told you how we are twins, brother from another mother is he. I have thought, too, something else: that we were of the Book of Revelation, chapter 11. That tells of two lampstands, which are two olive trees that stand before the Lord of the earth. I must say I coveted that position, pretty much from the first time I heard of it. I thought, those career opportunities are open, and there's only two of them, *and they're in the Bible!* That sounded simply awesome. So I thought we were it, him and me. (At the very least, I was told we were models to inspire other best friends by how we were. If we got nothing else, that would surely have been enough reward.)

Chapter 11 was not to be the case, however. Because I realized that during the transfiguration, when our Lord was still alive, Moses and Elijah *literally did* stand before the Lord of the earth (who, if you haven't guessed by now, is Jesus Christ). It was always them, not us. But in any event, Philip K. Dick and I *are* twins: we are red and blue, not the pink and light blue we originally saw: just the glow of light through us tinted these colors so. Red is traditionally the color of the Father, blue the color of the Son. So that does leave green, which is the color of the Spirit. And I found that it looks like we have a third, though I don't know how it fits: John the Baptist is the green one. Not sure how Philip K. and I deserve such company. But there you go, take it for what it's worth.

And then there is Joan of Arc, who has been with me from the beginning, when the visions began again in the summer of 1991. Sure, we had been friends all along, but I had this conception of her that she were like Jesus Christ or Newton: simply asexual. Then, just before there came this last round of vivid visions, there was at some point when I thought this whole other world in my mind were going away. When I was saying my goodbyes, I realized something, and I told her: out of everyone, I was going to miss her most of all. But whatever would be would be, n'est-ce pas? And then, after that and out of the clear bright blue, she asked me to marry her.

Huh. I was speechless for all of about 1 second. Me, who plays the lotto, was not going to let even the potential of this opportunity pass me by, so yeah, I said yes. This was actually how started the last round of visions, the end of the War in Heaven. I think because she inspired me throughout was how I was capable of performing the acts I did. She wasn't asexual at all, just a virgin for God, for what that meant when she was alive. And she became my third instance of what I have thought that it was true love. She was the first who touched on *The Princess Bride* rather than *Romeo and Juliet* (which is death, by the way). And which there was when I shared a simple moment with her, just talking, and that surpassed all the other moments of my life as THE BEST THERE EVER WAS. Wuv, twoo wuv...

You can sort of hear the Lord complaining sometimes, like, "Why do you call me Lord, Lord, and do not the things I say?" And this little note is especially for those who point their finger, and wag their heads (figuratively — I can't imagine anyone literally wagging his head in this day and age). Did he ever tell us to get in anybody else's business? Did he tell us to become as judgemental as we possibly could? I think I might guess that at this point, it would behoove us to ask what exactly he said for us to do. Ahem. Sure, there are moral proscriptions, some things he told us not to pursue, but when he was asked to summarize his entire teaching, he boiled it down to two things: love, and love. #1: Love God, and #2: Love one another. You were expecting...?

That's *love*, people. There in no way is any instruction to hate *anyone*. Even the haters — love even them. For God lets the sun shine on both the wicked and the just, both alike, and we must aspire to become perfect, like Him. Do you know what perfect is? It's love. Only love. Like that idea that the ancients had, about gods being the embodiments of ideals, like beauty or war. What if it's true, but there's only one thing, and it's *love,* baby? Like Einstein said, let us not get bogged down in this phenomenon, or that — let us know the mind of God. Yes, that would be love. Do I need to say it again? Cause if it takes you getting sick of hearing it to stick, I'm up for that. Love, love, love... love is all you need.[ix]

You know, every major religion has at the root the golden rule: do unto others as you would have them do unto you. This is a fact, backed by research. Do a little googling and you can find this to be so. It is not to say one religion is pretty much like another, but it is a key that many have found, just that one thing. I am, however, contractually bound to tell you that Christianity is the "correct" religion. Yes, I'm going to push my own religion on you to prove I'm just like the rest of them. Or maybe not? Because I have found two curious items that I don't know why they're not mentioned more in defending our particular faith.

Firstly, in Judaism, God says to Moses that His name is "I AM" — this is a brilliant conceit: no other god is named so, no other god *is*, this is saying. And no other god can have that name. By saying His name is "I AM", He is saying that God exists, I'm Him, and there is no other God. Period. And beyond that, the name Immanuel means, "God with us", which is saying that Jesus Christ, who has this name, is literally God in the form of a man. That is what being the Son of God means. So the messiah, which is what "Christ" means, must be the literal Son of God, which is what Christians believe him to be, with us on earth. The immanent God.

If you want to go further than that, we can see that from the behavior of the Son, since he shares the same nature as the Father, we may conclude that God is good, that God is love. For this is what the Son shows himself to be. He did not garner victory over evil by strength of might, friends. What would that have proven? He won by being the servant of all, put to death in an unjust world, giving his very life to bring salvation to that world, submitting to the will of God, whatever that might mean. The sign of Jonah, three days in the belly of the deeps. To overcome the world, to overcome death itself, for this is the Son of God: whose mystery is deeper than death. Put that in your pipe and smoke it.

Ultimately, your destiny is squarely in your hands. Once the Lord said to me a fascinating outlook, "What's unfair about life is that it *is* fair." This gave me tingles, and I thought it was the meaning of life, right there. (Turns out I didn't understand what the ultimate question is.) True, we do not get put on earth with exactly the same advantages as everyone else: some people have it easier, no doubt about that. Those who do have it easier will be the first to tell you that things *are* fair, if you factor everything into account. No. What the Lord was talking about was that everyone has the freedom to choose what one does with what is given. Whatever comes, it is up to you how you deal with it.

What a lot of people seem to be lacking is a simple attitude adjustment — right there, that can do wonders. Decide that you will not pass up the next opportunity that comes up: to do right, to do better, to do good. Not to waste whatever talent you may have in making excuses instead. Do you actually have any idea what it could possibly mean, to do your best? I would hope that the answer is no, unless you have done already some monumentally paradigm shifting feat in your life. Because that's what it means to do your best. Nobody is lacking that opportunity. Do something that will change, if not the world, then the whole of your life. Not all the time, but maybe at least once in the time you're given. And then, welcome to the team. We have a lot of work to do.

The women I've had relationships with... I'm definitely a legend in my own mind. *(Only* in my mind, though. Reality was always tougher.)* For one, I was pursued by and did myself pursue Rosanna Arquette for the longest time. What did Eris' Apple of Discord say? "For the prettiest"? Forsooth, that would be her, at least, circa 1987 or so. She came into the picture when the visions started, early on, in 1991. When I initially had thought I was talking to the same spirits of the people I saw as cartoons, as to be able to transmit and receive messages to their current earthbound forms, I ended up going to New York City a couple times to meet up with her because she said that she'd be there. Of course, those were just half baked, pipe dream journeys, but they were sort of fun, anyway.

I think she had that cultural issue that kept her from being attracted to Asians, so it was basically doomed from any start, right there. But at the time, I really believed that it was true love, and that we were bound together in a strange method. There was this one time that someone came closest to breaking us up: I was involved in some drama with her on the side: and that was Audrey Hepburn. But I remember, I couldn't help but introduce her as, "cultural icon", so that wasn't going to work, either. Years went on, and the woman in my head became a woman who was real, and she was a hottie, too; then she broke up with me, then we were back together, then not, but still present in my fantasy world, eventually to find out that on earth she'd married and had a baby. C'est la vie. Then I had a rebound relationship, in my mind, with a Russian model I knew, and then... and then... I was *found*. That was Joan of Arc. Quite a journey. Such is love, no?

I guess I should talk about the fourth member of my inner cabal, too (the other three: Jeanne, Phil, Arquette). I have had a friendship with Albert Einstein that has seen it all. It was known to go through a few troubles, mostly me being the one doing someone wrong — but not always. He was one of my closest friends, and though I spent probably the most time with him than any of my other three, I always saw him most as a colleague, a kindred spirit in science. He had the most input when I was working on my artificial intelligence. And metaphysics: I actually saw a mysterious thing, a black dot in my mind's eye, tiny, when we were discussing information and structure as what makes up the stuff of the cosmos. (I corrected him on a point there, whereupon the black dot popped up. And I don't think he ever forgave me for one-upping him then. The dot's meaning came later.)

Some people it was said thought of Albert as if he were not quite of this earth. That he seemed almost alien. Myself, I saw him quite differently: the most human human being that I'd ever met. And I mean human in the noblest of the meaning. (Why exactly do I have to say that? Are we really that bad, prototypically?) And you know, I loved him so much that I found a way to convert him to Christianity, just in case... but the Lord sort of made fun of me because I did: saying of him, "You didn't think we saved Einstein?" Sort of an incredulous tone, Yiddish accent. The implications, though, of that statement! You know what it means, right? Basically, He's saying, "We're going to save whomever we want to save." I say, "Whatever!" to your ideas that He must follow the letter of salvation's law! What do these poor relations know about love?

While I was in that room at that hospital, more of which trip I will get into further on, I had a vision of Satan being fought at the cross. The day was quite momentous in ways more than one. I felt the special circumstance of it being, the Holy Spirit strong in the air — there had been once before when such was applied to my person, years, decades before, that previous time looking like it were purposed for my awareness when such an event were occurring. It was just before, in that hospital, where I had been told that Judas had volunteered, though the exact wording was different than that, and I don't remember what it was.

I met Judas for the first time there in that room at the hospital, and he seemed a very capable saint. What I originally was allowed to believe about that statement, "Judas volunteered", was that it meant a horror beyond horrors. That he was heading into a vial where there would be no God, and that he were going to be without salvation, not even the mercy of a well-formed Hell. Something *worse*. These misunderstandings I would later see as being quite useful, like the "wrong" notes in jazz. And there was him in that confab with the higher ups, and I presume that Christ was there: yes, when he was told the plan to hand over our Lord. And there was reason why he would later have a hard time recalling this, quite after Satan had visited his mind, after the actual "betrayal" had happened.

And as I was thinking that what he was heading into was Cthulhu type eternal horror, he got ready to enter his vial. I found out later it was like unto armor to protect him from Satan during the handing over. Must have been *very* intense, the series of events of the "betrayal". But before he went, he gave me something to give John the Baptist (which I don't remember exactly what it was, it had something to do with emeralds), and he told me what sins I was to avoid further in my life. (I have kept to those things.) Then I saw his vial, then snap! He was gone, sealed therein. I felt something like desolation, for a fallen comrade, not understanding what was going on, like a twin in the womb when the other is born and gone out into the world. I was told he was smiling when he entered.

In Tolkien's *Ainulindalë* — in the creation of the world — Melkor, the greatest of the Ainur, introduces his own themes into the music primordial. It was therefore said that none of everything that existed on Middle Earth was of the exact form that was originally intended by the voices of the other Ainur, the heavenly beings, and that of Ilúvatar, who was God. I remember reading this and thought it was quite the interesting notion, which would explain *much* about the world at large: for there is much beauty, but which is much mixed with the ugly. I dismissed the notion, though, off hand, from having any truth in our own world. Surely Satan could not have had his hands *that deep* in the batter?

But then there was this one time, something I heard — almost overheard, almost an aside — that pain was not created by the God who is love. It was, rather, Lucifer's idea. Can I truly believe this? Because if this is THE WAY THINGS REALLY ARE, holy guacamole: how much would suddenly come into focus why things are the way things are. Pain was not invented by God, and if the myths are true, neither is sin, nor death. (Is sin actually pain?) Was this, then, what was the War in Heaven? To determine what and how things would be in the world, the universe, all creation? This was what we were fighting for? When Satan was cast into the earth, this was when he was no longer at his helm at the root controls of existence. These were the stakes. Glad I didn't know this much at the time. (That was mercy.)

The idea validates the notion of a world where we basically live by the rules made by the Devil. This was what was meant by the fact of Satan being Prince of said world, for this was the place where his hand was upon anything that is. I remember when I first had that thought, that the world was one which was *that* unfair — for just that reason — and upon the idea coming to the fore in my sulking, that we must live by the Devil's rules, I heard the Lord say, "Welcome to life." This was the world where God Himself was put *to death* after a life of HAVING DONE NOTHING WRONG. Where the best of us were tortured, and hanged, or worse, FOR BELIEVING; and it was easier to do the wrong thing than the right, to hate than love, to ignore than to care. And when we say things were meant to be, it is so more often than not by how well we pick up the pieces. *Welcome to life.*

My visions, I had many theories about what exactly I was looking at. I call it HALOSPACE because it doesn't depend on anyone else's definition — that just means, whatever I see. At one point, however, I liked to call what I saw as watching the Dreaming. Not only because of the Australian aborigines' conception of such a space (which I really haven't done enough research to relate to it, anyway), but it seemed to make so much sense, for the common definition of the word: something had made my dreaming invade my waking world. That which was in my unconscious spilled into the conscious, as if there were like a small and persistent leak. That's why I had thought to say that the people I saw were just the people you meet in dreams.

So, it wasn't really happening, in this line of reasoning; none of it was "real". None of it was in the deepest cuts relevant to what was going on in "real life" — it would all blow over, just wait. Or you could say, considering in what circumstances it all started, it was just a trip… And then, the conditions for what I was seeing changed. Drastically and irreversibly. Now, it *has* to be happening in some way — it must at some fundamental level be real. That vision I had where Satan was cast from Heaven *must have happened.* There are no two ways about it. All that led up to it, the preparations, and the vision itself, have a verisimilitude that rationally, can only lead to the thought that what I saw was what I saw. More on this later.

There is so much you take for granted, that if you wrote them down, surely they would fill all the books in the world. What *I* take for granted, they would fill a few less, because I have pondered such a thing as how not to take the barest functioning of anything for granted. The reason for that I explained before, one of those cases of where the curse *is* the blessing; but that sidenote notwithstanding, just like a fish doesn't know what water is, you generally don't understand just how much you should really, really be thankful for. For example, we can take just one of our senses, and just one aspect of that sense: seeing color.

In *The Color Purple* is written how God gave us the delight of the eponymous color purple, and well should we be in wonderment about such a thing. But take the least of all colors, if any can be said to be so; perhaps beige: and see how fantastic it is that we can have light that has an emotion (such is color), and that we can experience it. Fantastic. The fact that there are three primary colors that must mix in a particular way to give you that particular shade. That there is a medium through which that color, over there, can travel the distance to meet your eyes. How your eyes can perceive color at all, and that we sense its particularity by countless firings of neurons that make up conscious thought. That light travels and is not stationary. That distance is traversable. That time ticks forward to let things happen... Do you yet see that there are numberless things that make up the least of *any* experience?

When we try to examine why things are as they are, in the noble pursuits of science, we try and take one by one thing less as an assumption. We try and explain why something happens, and we take one less thing for granted. (We cannot explain yet why it is we can explain things, however. To be revisited.) If you are careful in the chain you follow, you can always, at any level, ask why a certain thing is a certain way instead of some other way. It appears that such lines of questioning can be infinite. So, what does it mean, then, to ask indeed, "What if it keeps going?" (The lines of questions, that is. This point gets further treatment later, in a discussion I had with Einstein.) I say, if it does keep going, and going, then ultimately, what we have is a transcendent phenomenon; and only if it ever does stop dead in that chain of "why" somewhere, is the universe, is creation, ultimately meaningless. And seeing *all* these reasons, that go on and on and on: we take all but an infinitesimal of them as given, as part of the system, not brought to mind... and there is a reason for that.

With even worlds enough and time, we will *never* be able to answer it all, *especially* if it is true that we can always ask why. This is not to say that science is without use; on the contrary, this means science will always be of use. Always to discover why something is as it is, if there always is a reason. It speaks of more things in heaven and earth, Horatio, than are dreamt of in your philosophy...[x] We have the barest toehold on what things are, why things are, how they came to be and how their future will progress. And we *cannot but* take the sum of the great masses of reasons for granted, except for the shallowest of scratches: for we are mere mortal frailty, none of us capable of gathering to mind the sublime coherence of all rationale, dive the timeless depths of meaning held in even a single color, unreflected — the most normal thing in the world.

I have seen snakes in the fire. No, this is not a portent of doom. It was in a commercial on TV, the view from the top of a fire a few feet wide. I think it was actually a commercial for charcoal; now I don't remember. There was a grill and it was the charcoal that was in flames — nothing weird, but interesting to display a screenful of fire as the central image for your product. But it happened to be the case that I was coming back into the real world from a little stint in a mental institution. So, a little tweaked, would we? (Ahem. Kidding around.) The licking of the flames looked like snakes slithering. Snakes made of the flickering plasma-like sliptwisting of fire in curving fluctuation. Nothing much really came of that vision, just a really cool thing to witness.

Also, while we're on the subject, I saw once when I looked at one of van Gogh's self-portraits, the yellows and oranges: it looked like that paint was on fire. There are other things I have seen, too, but these two stand out in the more or less hallucinatory side of this whole experience. And people may think of madness as being dark, but I found that the opposite was much rather the case: things being supernaturally bright was more of the indicator of insanity. So anyway, there were other things which may not have been so flashy as these two in aspects of fire, but some of the more subdued ones — those may have portended things of quite the deeper scope.

(In which I have sometimes found myself walking through a dream, day through day. I do not know if you would call it all madness, though I know that there were things I have been through that would most definitely qualify. Sometimes to feel like that song:

> i am superman, and i know what's happening
> i am superman, and i can do anything...[xi]

I've had that feeling, I don't know whether it is so very good or so very bad, that I am a hero upon the world, who does great things in the service of humanity. I know it is not just a dream, these visions of mine; I know it is not just a passing madness, that flows into the backwaters of time, never to be questioned or rationalized. I think madness has not the poetry that I have witnessed, the verse of musical meanings that have sewn in me such hope, that I will never wear a mind without the fabric so intimate with love, love intrinsic in the thread. There is a light. Try to walk in it. That is what my visions say.)

The Church of the Subgenius is a tongue-in-cheek religion that may or may not be serious. They correctly point out that when some off color group does arise that *is* serious, they're at a high risk for elimination. With prejudice. A bunch of Subgenius related themes have presented themselves in my visions, the primary being that on several occasions did I meet J. R. "Bob" Dobbs (its head (and also have I occasioned to meet the anti-Bob)). I once concluded since he was an imaginary entity, he was the only real thing that I was seeing in my visions (the rest being figments of fantasy, since they were representative of things in the real world in some way — that is prime Subgenius logic).

He is foremost a prophet of God, a truly fascinating character. No nonsense, great sense of humor. I once asked him, in all honesty, "Why do you do what you do?" And he really had to put his mind to it. Being a rather perfect servant of God, I don't think it ever entered his mind to ask. Finally, he answered, "I'm a good guy." That was it: because he was one of the good guys; this was his raison-d'être. Simple, noble. That would be Bob. Like on Albert Einstein, I performed an unnecessary conversion on him to Christianity. I actually sold the greatest salesman in the world on

Jesus. Or you know, maybe not, could've been that he was always a believer. Sometimes you wonder what's actually going through his head. I imagine something divine.

Atheists, and perhaps some other groups, believe that ultimately, there is no purpose to the world except that we give meaning to it. Well intentioned, very rational, but it seems also to touch the height of arrogance. To think that there is no purpose to such beauty, on the grandest scales, except what human beings tag it, with our crude implements of language, music, art, etc.: seriously, that's the best that can be made of these incredible vistas? Or could it be otherwise, that skeptics are actually humbled by the magnificence of the great things of the universe? To those who have eyes to see, it is exactly like the hypothesis that there must be other life in the universe because of the sheer number of other worlds that must be out there. There is so much beauty that there *must be* a greater purpose.

A lot of argument by materialists (those who only believe in what they can physically touch) boils down to one possibility: things may be this way because they *have to be* this way. There might be no other way it could work. This line of reasoning also accounts for the thought that there might be other universes, with other laws of physics, just that this one is the one where things work enough for us to observe that it does. We will visit this notion again. It then may come down to a variation of the Anthropic Principle: things work this way because we cannot conceive of any other way they *would* work. But let me tell you, I've glimpsed Heaven, and it *doesn't* have to work this way. There is infinite possibility in material, that which we might have difficulty in visualizing because they only work by a certain means here. There are different ideas of physics than we can conceive of, because our brains just don't go in that direction, so we rather can't even *think* of conceiving them.

It comes down to taking things for granted. Again. And to think that all that you see is all there is. We do not think that there is a greater purpose, a Heaven to this earth, because we ignore that which evinces such a purpose. Can you conceive that all you see might not be all there is? One believes in the existence of Africa because it fits in the framework of logic that lets us conceive of its existence without our having to go there. The spiritual world is different, indeed: there seems to be no grand framework that governs what goes on, where you can go, who you can talk to, and how any of these things happen. The thing is, it can't be made sense of the way things make sense in the material world. That is the flaw in trying to find its governing dynamics. One might think, however, given the sheer number of people who have experienced this *other,* that one might give a second thought to dismissing it offhand.

I say it is possible to touch this unseen world for yourself, and to see that it is real, after all. Because there are people who have gone there and come back, and for all the different types of visions they have seen, we all have the same commonality that we are human beings, every one of us, who can only express things in terms of our 5 basic senses. Let us then say this entire book is a method by which God is reaching down into the earth, which it is. Can you conceive of a logic by which all that is spoken of here is true? For surely all of it is to the best of my recollection that which was real, to me. And if you do let in *that* possibility, you then touch the unseen world thereby (or it touches you, equivalently). See if that makes any difference, any at all, in your life.

I do know what people think, and I have thought so, too, I will admit. I wrote on a blog about how in 1997 I realized that everything I had been experiencing was just psychosis; I wrote that that was winning a hardfought battle... with my mind, I suppose... As I said, before this last set of visions, I would get somewhat blasted out of my mind, after having done drugs, then I would come down, get medicated, and I would think it was all "just a trip". So what if none of these things happened, and I never met Albert Einstein, or Joan of Arc, or the Archangel Michael? To think, again, what if it *was* just the dream mechanism in the mind that broke, and it was nothing more *than* a waking dream, and there is no reality to such things outside one's own mind?

The thing is, I have seen things that cannot be so easily explained. More than once, I have seen the future. I have been able to predict what was about to happen. More often than not, if I try and do such prophesying, it's wrong, but if there is a certain tone to the thought, it happens as foreseen previous to the happening. (There is one prediction, one prophecy that I make: as of writing this, in 2013, things, worldwide — they're about to take off. This is not the end, this is the beginning, of a grand prosperity. Fantastic things are about to happen.) I cannot discount the visions so lightly. And as everyone who has seen miraculous things will tell you, *I know what I saw.* (Comes with, when other people say, "Couldn't it have been just an XXX?" to reply, "Do you think I'm an idiot?")

Yes, the visions started while I was on drugs. Not this last time though; when they took me over this time, I was on nothing. Not even cold medicine. And what do these visions of Jesus Christ and His angels do to me? They make me live a better life, they make me *believe.* So you can explain it as me having hallucinations that act just like Jesus and His angels should act, doing what they should be doing, to help me be like a saint is supposed to be, and then to say, "but they're not real" — when does it become irrational *not* to believe? Because I passed that point some while back. If you say that such things are not possible, I ask you, how on earth have you come to know all things with such certainty? And, why are you not going around in a van solving crimes?

I am an annihilationist. This means I do not believe in an eternal Hell, where the wicked are punished infinitely for a finite amount of sin. That never really made sense to me. I believe that when the netherworld is tossed (with its inhabitants) into the Lake of Fire, all of them are burned so that nothing of them remains, as painful as the amount of sin they committed in life would warrant. For He told us that the wages of sin is *death,* not torment. I don't know what twisted definition of death you have, because it seems to me to be meant as cessation of existence. And an eternal Hell *is definitely not death.* When the Lord mentioned Gehenna, that was where garbage was burnt up *and nothing was left*. We follow the advice of Augustine, and not the Bible, to believe in an eternal Hell. To repay one soul's errors with the suffering of the totality of creation's evil is the point where God ceases to be called love. For that's what an infinite suffering means.

Simply put, the question of whether to side with good vs. evil is merely to ask if you can get along with everyone else. If you consistently cause harm, consistently show complete disregard for everyone else, that answer would be no. So, you don't want to be a part of eternity, then? OK, pay your debts and you're history. No muss, no fuss. And about the passage in Revelation about Satan twisting in agony forever and ever? A different translation is that actually is for an age and ages that he burns — a lot, but that would be as expected for the prime evil. He has caused many lifetimes of pain, after all. But at the end, he would be no more, as well. And I know I may be wrong, but this seems like such a sensible way of God's justice to be manifest, you know? Thus do I believe.

There are two significant questions to any human being's life: "What do you do?" and "Why do you do it?" The correct answers (yes, there are correct answers) are, "I serve God," and "Because I love life." And if you don't believe in God, then the answers become that you serve a nobler purpose, a greater purpose than what you are, what is larger than you; and that you do it because you love life. You know what these larger things are, I need not tell you of them. Think Doctors Without Borders. One understands that the defaults, in fact, are "I work," and "To pay the bills." But if the profession you follow is done to finance your existence, that does not preclude that you can serve God as well. And it doesn't mean you can't, or even *shouldn't* love life.

Because Dostoevsky defined human as "biped, ungrateful" is exactly why you should have these two answers in your repertoire. If you don't see all that you should be grateful for, if you truly cannot see past the things that didn't go right, the things you couldn't have, the love that didn't work out, the dreams that were crushed, let me be Clarence the angel to your George Bailey. Yes, *It's a Wonderful Life*. If you look, you will see that you are

48

equipped to handle all the bad stuff that comes your way, even to make those bad things turn out good.

I understand that life doesn't always work out. But you can find your footing if you stumble, you can get back up again when you fall. I tell you things you have heard already: the trap is only in your mind. So is any defeat. You are free, human, as long as you can still love in response to any wrong. You cannot fail if what you do, no matter what, is love. Because if you can do that, then you have won, no matter what any record book says. If you have been through some really horrible stuff: let me first say that I don't really understand how bad those things were; but let me tell you, too, that God *does.*

Have you ever seen videos of children who brave things like cancer and congenital heart disease? It really puts things in perspective. You will feel like a piece of crap if you've just been complaining about how someone dinged your car door after looking at that kind of courage. Love life. Even the suffering is the good stuff, sometimes. (That's called, "Count it all joy.") And when you do love life, you will want to serve God, or serve some bigger purpose. *This cannot be wrong.* If you are reading this, most likely you have never known what it is like to starve. You can read and write. You have a brain. You have a heart. See what you can do with a little focus: and if and when you amaze yourself, be thankful for that, too.

So, the last time I ended up in a mental institution, that day, I had been put through my paces in Angel Proving Grounds, which did look like NYC, but there were definitely *differences* to earth. I remember quite clearly, for one, that the walk and don't walk electric signs were not a little white man walking and orange hand halting. They were strange alien sigils, abstract in form. Anyway, it ended with a trip in an ambulance because someone saw me huddled alone at night before a closed storefront and thought I might be having a stroke. I was cold (it was January, which I mistakenly said that it was July, I was so far out there) and for the last time, I thought I had blown it all; I thought I was irretrievably lost, for one final instance.

So, nice and warm in New York Presby, the hospital I have previously mentioned — before I was sent to the mental place — I was lying there, when some of the angels (Michael's angels) related to me what some of the things they went through on the front lines of the War were like. Basically, what is reality? What if, if *any* of Michael's angels failed, the world would have become irrecoverably deranged, fundamentally illogical? Flawed, and wrong? And this is what it *means* to be an angel of God: when the stakes are that high, *you do not fail.* Whatever that might mean, whatever effort you have to put out, whatever humiliation, blasphemy, feces, *whatever* that means you have to endure, or have thrown at you, *you do it.* Because there literally is *no other option.*

The derangement Satan and his angels tried to perpetrate touches once more on how we take so much for granted — for instance, logic and consistency. What if you could not take some very fundamental things as certainties? For instance, if you have 8 things arranged in a rough circle, you can count on there being 8 spaces between them. What if you couldn't? What if there were only 7? Or 6? What if you were trapped in something and needed to get out of one of those spaces, and the seeming escapes were not reality? Because there were pockets of the derangement, as they were being in attempt to inflict upon reality, in the War in Heaven, that existed enough to be dangerous, harmful at least to the angels that fought them. All of which had ramifications, high and low, to the very foundations of existence. In other words, it was as if Atlas, the titan who held up the sky, were being attacked...

There have been some extraordinary visions I have had. Once God the Father showed me of what stuff Heaven is made. Along with that vision, I glommed a thing or two about what exactly was possible in There, during the War. I cannot, that is I cannot now summon the ability, to tell you how wonderful that place is, being God's throne, whereas earth is merely His footstool. He also gave me an idea about what the proper usage of His name is, that of Yahweh. It is a holy name, and there is a reason you do not take the LORD's name in vain. For one, saying you do things in the name of someone means you invoke their authority. Names carry such weight. Now pretend that a name is weightier than the whole of creation, seen and unseen. And carries more power. If that seemed a little scary, *that is the correct reaction.* If not, you might look into what grade level your reading comprehension stopped at.

Outside those special visions, you know I have had mostly a desaturated view, cartoonish, of the goings on in HALOSPACE. Outlines, partial cartoons (enough so that I can tell just what they depict), usually shades of just one color. I joke, color-coded for my convenience. Yellow generally for Christ-like things, blue for more secular/normal things that are of good, and red or black tends to be bad guy stuff. They're not always that way, and when they aren't, I'm usually told so, and maybe why. Silently, through the angelic circuitry. The angels (and Jeanne d'Arc, too) tell me lots of things. I have not always been able to correctly gauge things for what they are, but my talent apparently is having the intestines that make from "garbage in", "a pearl of great price". You just need patience, and a lot of layers to sacrifice. So mote it be.

Philip K. Dick described God as being found in the trash layer of the world. This struck me as having a high content of truth. What are we to make of that statement? Why would this be? For is not God found above the highest heaven? Indeed, is not Heaven God's throne, and earth merely a footstool? Yet I look back, when He visited this world, and showed His true nature. He came not to rule, but to serve, the reason why almost all the Jews rejected Him as the messiah. He was the opposite of what they were expecting — the Suffering Servant, not the conquering king. This, too, I find thinking has a significant quality of truth to it. In the very nature of nature we find the surprises that now we don't think about, like the great dinosaurs all dying out and the Lilliputian rodent-like mammal sweeping over as the victor of evolution (for now). Now we do not find it at all unusual that an image of a crucified man, we use to give us strength. Selah.

After the shouting as He rode on a donkey, "Hosanna in the highest!", what happened then? This is God, your King, o people, come down from on high. This is God with us, our Immanuel. We have waited so long for our Savior to come, and now He comes in peace into the City of Prophets, the city of the Presence, the Temple. Do we make Him, then, King over all the earth? For God so loved the world, that He gave us this man, His only begotten Son, so that whosoever believes in Him, it is as if that soul were never to die, even if they were to leave this green world. What can we possibly do for such a man, who saves us even from our own selves? For being the Son of God *means* that He is God, for one God there is, and so the Son of God must share God's very nature. God with us.

Must it be that the stone the builders rejected become the cornerstone? What is to be if He were given to the archons of the Temple, the elders? Will they not pay Him tribute? Or will they pass Him along to become like a curse, and "for the good of the many, is one sacrificed"? (I'm cold, I'm cold...)[xii] What do they say has the crowd demanded, if it can be believed? One thinks it no small thing that those who cheered this King of the Jews now turn away, afraid. Who are we, now, leading Him to His final fate, through the streets of Jerusalem? (I'm cold, I'm cold...) Who is it now, who asks for forgiveness for those who slay Him? Who is being raised upon a tree, upon a cross? Who have we crucified, for all of the world and people and eternity and angels to see? Who? (I'm cold, I'm cold...) It is God. And we have thrown him away....

At times I have had to stop, take a second, and shake myself and say, "Yes, John H. Doe, this is really happening." Sometimes that was not enough, and one of the higher ups had to do it. Jesus Christ interrupted my regularly scheduled reality to break in and say so to me. I don't know if it is actually easier for me to believe that some of these things are happening than for someone else who is clued in to what exactly is possible in the paradigms I play in. What is real is real, no matter how much it resembles an hallucination. What Philip K. described as reality: that which, once you stop believing in it, it doesn't go away. Doesn't help the schizophrenics, though, who desperately *want* to stop believing in the things they hear and see, but are simply unable to. And I have been diagnosed with that, if you must know; but some people will also will diagnose Joan of Arc and the prophet Ezekiel with it, too. Surely not *all* of us are mad?

The skeptic in me (the scientist, I like to think) still wants to label everything I see as a figment of my imagination. Which I'm sure many, if not most of you out there are wont to do. I completely understand. But, my goodness, what I have *seen!* I cannot pragmatically consider that my imagination, with schizophrenia supercharging it even, is so grand to have conjured up just everything that have been in my visions. (I have seen INFINITY!) What is pride here, what is the humility? To believe I have been given a mind so great to be capable on its own, to have such visions? Or that I have been blessed by a touch of God, to be given these sights and sensations? No win situation? No lose situation? On a profound high, I am, to see so where horizons lead.

One interesting vision I had was of how the elements gain their characteristics. It appeared in my mind while I was in Brooklyn, at a Throbbing Gristle concert, which I was invited to by my Russian friend, Boris. We had just had dinner, and I had had a drink during, plus I was taking some cold medicine. So, on something of an altered state of mind, I saw the various elements in simple models, and what different electron "shells" they had ("shells" in quotes because it is a rather antiquated concept, but one that best describes how we can understand an atom's interface). We realize that, with very few exceptions, one only interacts with an atom via those "shells". The nucleus pretty much only gives an atom its mass.

If we understand that elements behave the way they do, when encountering other elements or more of the same element, because of the structure of their electron "shells", we understand the façade of this emergence to be the fundamental structure to what qualitatively we experience of any substance at all. The factors that are determined by placement of electrons emerge by their bonding to other elements, or the same, and the resultant molecular arrangements make emergent larger scale behavior and qualities of elemental substance and molecular structures. The devil is in the details, God is the God of small things. That is how fine tuned the qualities are of that which we call physical reality: the humming of the electrons sing into being all of creation.

For those who might be wondering about my motive for writing this book, ulterior or no, let me just say I am not trying to formulate an airtight argument for the existence of God or the salvation of our Lord Jesus Christ. Nor am I trying to invent some simplistic mechanism for conversion, à la Pascal's Wager. It is often fruitless to try and convert someone who does not actively seek after such an experience. I *am* trying to make it *scientifically plausible* that in fact, God does exist, and that Jesus Christ was Him. (To restate, being the Son of God does mean one *is* God. The elders at His trial say the blasphemy is that "this man says he is God.") Note that I am not saying "possible", but "plausible". We're trying to reach over the 50% line of probability, if we can.

It is prelimarily to acknowledge that first, God may possibly exist. If you don't even admit that possibility, you're just as bad as the religious fundamentalists, and I bid you good day. Then, we talk about the prophets: these are the men (and women) who basically had God's phone number. Why doesn't God talk to us directly? The Bible actually addresses this question. Apparently, *that* is a terrifying experience (the Israelites begged Moses and God that He should speak only through Moses after they had gotten a full on blast of Radio Yahweh). The prophets tell us that God does exist, though their picture of Him is necessarily incomplete, and their views of the "unseen" world are colored by their own imaginations.

Then we have Jesus Christ. Not to bad mouth Buddha or Muhammad, but neither of them claimed to be God, so these two must be basically still be in the wading pool with the other prophets, no matter how far in the deep end of that they want to go. Jesus Christ was the Son of God. That means 1) He was perfect, 2) He was eternal, 3) He was, in fact, God. I cannot stress this last point enough. This means, being infinite, He could render Himself to be the only necessary sacrifice that covered the wrongdoings of all of humanity, through all of time. And that He had a direct wire to the transcendent God — a line that death itself could not break — and therefore, He was able to come back from the dead on His very own. No one else had such a connection. How is this scientifically plausible? If we say that God is possible, then we are free to believe this man, who *told us* He was God. And because He did everything we might conceive such a being would do — by this evidence, it therefore *becomes* plausible, all the claims about Him. By Him and His actions we may indeed believe that God *is* love. 1... 2... 3... ∞.

For one, I can see what doubters see. Myself, I was a devout atheist for many of my days, earlier on. In college I debated believers into the ground. Why should we believe in a man in the sky, rather than, say, a flying spaghetti monster? What's the difference between believing in God rather than believing unicorns? Are they not both far fetched? To them I say, God confounds the wise with what is plain to children. For true it is that nowadays the wisest among us just may be these atheists, and secular humanists. They who do not count on another, next world, and instead count on this as our only existence. (And shame on the "children of God" for not acting as some of those do, and smugly count on God to vindicate them.)

We must think that it is not so preposterous. Outrageous claims must produce outstanding evidence. We know there is no evidence that a flying spaghetti monster (FSM) had any hand in the creation of the universe. We do, however, have evidence that there is a God, whose name is Yahweh, who had a Son, whose name is Jesus Christ (by the way, it is correct to say "Christ" is part of his name). No one is supposed to believe in the FSM, but believing in the Lord: this actually gives one a clearer picture of WHAT IS ACTUALLY GOING ON. And that is why you should believe. As far as evidence, to a corrupt generation will only be given the sign of Jonah, who was three days in the belly of the whale. The evidence is Jesus Christ's resurrection, which most would say is part of the claim. No, sir. If and when the Lord calls you to Him, your eyes will be opened. See if then, that doesn't set you free, for no truth is truth that does not set you free!

So as far as books and their titles go, we may reasonably claim that this one is a gospel, the word meaning, literally, "good news". It was applied to the now normally termed Gospels because they proclaimed the good news of Jesus Christ. If you haven't noticed, this is one of those types of books. Now, the "according to Judas". Well, if we take the most positive interpretation about the names of the four canonical Gospels, their "according to XXX" means what is thought XXX would tell us of the good news. Because it is scholarly belief that Matthew, Mark, Luke, and John did not, in fact, write their eponymous gospels. In a cynical interpretation about these names and their claims, perhaps some people believed that using the names belonging to the "in group" would lend authority to the books that were written, while the original writers had not been from that group.

Not totally separate from that group, though, if one can be a little kind. They who wrote the canonical Gospels obviously were members of the faith; these were definitely not written by atheists or non-Christian Jews, certainly not by the Essenes. Most likely, they believed that the writing of those Gospels was their mission, and perhaps the specific people who filled out their "according to" had special meaning to them. And so it is with me. A believer on a mission, who is telling the Good News of Jesus Christ, because perhaps the old Gospels need a little more help, these days, to be as enlightening as they used to be. And Judas? I certainly do have a special reason for using his name to fill out my "according to". Judas is a friend of mine. And I know the truth of his name: no evil lies there.

It was during a discussion I was having with Einstein (about reasons why) that the question popped up, which I have mentioned before. We were talking about how "why this" begat "why that," and "why that" begat another why. Both at the same time, we asked, "What if it keeps going?" Both from the opposite perspective on the question if God necessarily existed. When I asked the same question as he did, he knew that he had lost the argument. So, the point was, if there are always reasons why, what place is there for God? He seems unnecessary if we can always find the why of why. Which brings back the point of either it's ultimately meaningless, or ultimately transcendent. If there is no God, it is the former: if there is no ultimate answer, then we are, at the final count, without mattering.

We can without God seem to live purposeful lives, ones with things like science at the helm to provide us with meaning, like to live for the preservation and furtherance of life. But if at every step in reasoning why, all we are left with is questions, there is no ultimate substance to all the reason. If, on the other hand, you begin and end with "God is love," we then do have the beginning and end: of being itself. Albert seemed to have forgotten one thing he had said, while he was alive: "There are two ways to live: you can live as if nothing is a miracle; you can live as if everything is a miracle." And really, any miracle is of God, however rationally you may comprehend its existence. And God's omniscience: that is to know the answer to every question why, even if it keeps on going, before the question is ever asked.

If you believe, then you must believe this: that whatever evil, it will inevitably play into the purpose of God. This, I think, is the most difficult point to reconcile, and perhaps the key to the entire puzzle of existence. It is where, I think, we have the sticking point that people simply cannot reconcile, the point where some fall away from faith entirely. For it is a deep point of conviction in the greatness of God, and in His wisdom: that no matter how horrible, how horrific, that He can make of it right: if not in the immediate now, somewhere "in the end" (vague but sure). It is something we *must* believe, we of the faith, or the entire faith ceases to be nothing more than a band-aid on a sucking wound.

It may be that there are just too many things in the world that test this hypothesis. There are too many things that can shake this heart of belief. The true believer must be able not to turn away from the worst of the evil in the world, and still in his soul believe that God is good. Supremely good. For the greater the horror, the greater the God we must believe in — for only One *greater* than the evil can exist, if He exists at all. If making us believe that he does not exist is Satan's greatest trick, surely it is at least his secondmost favorite ploy to make of the world a playground of horrors. For anyone who feels, it makes faith need to explain itself. And God seems so silent on such things. But that is the test.

The following just came to me one sunny day, and the Lord remarked that it was the best thing I'd ever written:

> *There was a light, but it faded. It was not faith.*
> *There were visions, but they twisted. They were not*
> *   faith.*
> *There was a feeling, but it was illusory. It was not*
> *   faith.*
> *Faith was to hold on, when all those things went*
> *   wrong.*
> *Because I saw that light, had those visions, felt what I*
> *   felt.*
> *The narrow way is a journey, and rest may only be*
> *   momentary.*
> *It is a life that leads to life.*

It didn't all make sense until later, for I had written it years before the War's end, and only leading up to and through that end did it completely reveal itself. It is a way to keep faith in this continually shifting sphere we call life, where nothing seems secure. You don't have to discard the old things because you outgrow them in some way. You may believe in the same way as an angel, whose faith is constant in change, the flux of pure spirit, and is therefore touched of the eternal.

In a passing moment in the Dreaming, once, outside of sleep and in my visions: I from this certain perch perceived the notion, conceived of a very curious thing. Originally not even put into words I could hear, but existing as a partially conceived cartoon and almost purely semantic in thought, thus no words enclosing: "the Tree of the Forgetting of the Knowledge of Good and Evil." Has anyone else conceived of something that could be so wondrous? I cannot think that this idea has ever occurred to anyone ever before; such a thought in my reckoning would catch on in certain circles, would it not? Bottles of virginity? A lollipop of purity? Youth, just the good parts? The splash of being new again.

The claim of thus imagined is nothing less than the return to innocence, a return to Eden. When we were naked, and were not ashamed. Such fruit I imagined to be heart-shaped, and bright yellow — a fresh sweetness, no hint of sour at all. Almost as if skinless. And to eat of it, the sensation I cannot think of what it might be like. Better than childhood. Wider to the eye than an open sky.

Sing the song that songs cannot sing. Write the words that words cannot say. Draw what cannot be pictured, dance in ways the body cannot go. Find the inspiration for it all from the God who is love, for love is the greatness that greatness aspires to. The eternal that lives in our mortal souls.

Thus is our true purpose in anything worth doing: to do the impossible. Can anything less be what is meant for us all, for the children of God? See how wonderful is the creation of our Father, and dream that we may also do such things as our Father is responsible for — when we are ready. When we know enough, when we have done enough. In eternity we will see what that means. Our second birth will be when we are born anew in Heaven, and will we there grow up to be as children of God are meant to be. Can we expect anything less of ourselves, we children of the light, made in the image of love, than what is love's true potential? To do in all justice what cannot be done?

(Do not say "cannot". We will forget such words.)

---

i hear tell there is a flower
which blooms only in the darkness:

59

if light were displayed upon it
would it immediately turn to dust.
now, how it is it may be
i have heard but scant the rumors,
rare few who faintly claim
they have seen what the flower
in its cool nethers may be...
palest of the white petals
which seem to be suspended
in air, so gossamer is its stalk...
these folk who breathe the subject
of this invisible, impossible flower,
others whisper they were born
and were nourished there,
in blackness deeper than night:
better to view the mysteries
of life, of flowers only darkness sees.

What if, at the end of the day, Romeo and Juliet were *not* meant for each other? And it was exactly this quality that made them what they were? What if "meant to be" is actually really boring, and what that really is is all the people who got together without the drama, married and had kids, who had kids, and they grew old, and died, and that was the whole story? When the entire world is against you, after dropping hint after hint, what you get is one stolen night, and then that entire world catches up to you — death is almost inevitable. Some sort of horrible tragedy, at least. But that's *Romeo & Juliet,* right? There is no way it would have been anywhere near as romantic had they not both died at the end, being a hairsbreadth from getting away with the perfect crime.

Whether this means that it was true love, after all, or that it was not, is just because when one thinks of true love, one's mind immediately jumps to the concept "meant to be" — maybe I'll leave that as an exercise for the reader. Is this an example of love's true nature? I think not. It is an exception, and that is precisely why it is so prized as a story, as an experience. Maybe I am leaning in one direction, then. One idea of true love: if you love, truly, what else need it be? When you say, "I love you," are you telling the truth? That's it then. Maybe that's all true love is meant to be. The nature of the world can be seen in this way, too: that the most ordinary of people can experience the most extraordinary of phenomena. For free. And I rather like that way of looking at the world.

There comes over some of us, sometimes, a notion that perhaps should always be shared, if one is so fortunate to experience it. It is the idea that everything is going to be all right — that somehow, beyond the reach of all mortal hopes, everything will at the end, end well. Is it so hard to believe?

Though those who have religion have more form to these feelings, a spelled-out prophecy or some kind of formulation that actually describes how things will work out, I don't believe one has to believe in anything to believe this. I imagine it is somewhat more easily done for those who have faith in a higher order to believe that there is a larger good that circumscribes the most terrible of tragedies, but hope is not monopolized by such faith. There shall always be those who have a kind of trust in the better side of humankind, no matter that they can only look forward to new generations to make amends for those past (and those present) and think not that some great power will create the ultimate justice. This is not an impossible thing to hold. Hope asks not for your credentials.

It is, to put it in today's parlance, the ultimate meme. We can see that it's been put in songs more than once (Bob Marley's "No Woman No Cry" says it, for one; do a search for "everything's gonna be alright" on Google, and you get more than twenty million hits). And it probably shall be put into songs as long as there are songs being written. To those who don't feel it, perhaps have never felt it, the idea may be shrugged off as lighthearted wish-fulfillment whimsy, made by those who have no grasp of how grave the situation of the world truly is. But that it exists in such forms as the Book of Revelation, I think says differently. It is perhaps to be as in the spirit of a quote by Oscar Wilde, "The mystery of love is greater than the mystery of death." That to fight the good fight is ultimately not in vain, however much the evil seems victorious. It is the idea of turning the other cheek: they cannot defeat us by their violence; we are better than that. It is a sign that says, "This way up." Everything is going to be all right.

> there are zero matadors
> dancing on zero tables
> fighting zero ferocious bulls
> zero bloodthirsty spectators
> carried by zero flying carpets
> yelling zero metaphysical truths
> and the zero of the countdown
> makes much of such nothings
> as zero approaches in secret
> the flip of a dread switch
> when everything happens
> and the crowd goes wild
> at the slaying of the bulls
> while the matadors dance
> while we fly into oblivion

Somehow, we must remove the notion from us of our own infallibility. It is a hindrance like no other. Somehow we can discern the faults of everyone but our own selves, because we always have a reason why this or that thing of ours went afoul, so that we seem always to be justified. Do you see that to live purely in the echo chamber of our rationalizations is literally to become an idiot?

We must constantly strive to see the right in everyone else, and see the wrong in us, because the balance is *always* stacked the other way. Our selves will always get in the way of any selfless notion — by their definitions, this must be the case. There was only ever one of us who did nothing wrong, and I think on the day of judgement, we will be surprised — shocked — by the amount and number of the ills we have rendered, the injustices we were responsible for that we have overlooked, all the while pointing at the mote in our brothers' eye, seeking all that we thought was unfair to us to be rectified, and all that which we did of the dishonorable overlooked. Stupidity and madness. I do not think this will be how the Judge will look at things, who sees all, dispassionate. Who is judgement's judgement, and KNOWS why you did what you did…

Of course, at times I have my doubts about this whole Judas thing. It's natural. Barring the "Gospel of Judas", very little has been written that is favorable about him. The Gospels themselves paint him with the same brush as they do to lacquer the Antichrist, calling *only those two* "son of perdition". Only from personal experience do I know that Judas is held in the Lord's favor, nothing written do I consult for such an opinion (I have never read the Gospel of Judas, but know *of* it and that it is a Gnostic book, and has the same problems with it as many other Gnostic works). And what I believe goes counter to the official position, basically held everywhere, of Judas' wickedness. I think perhaps Judas himself has a similar problem as I had, for I have seen that Satan really did a number on him; the Lord seems to keep reminding him that He *told* Judas to hand Him over. And Judas stares back with sort of a glazed expression when He does.

But I am in a unique position to hold this knowledge, and I will not let it go if I possibly *can* hold onto it. I do not know what Satan did to him, especially if it drove such a strong man to kill himself, but I have been through situations where I thought I was the other "son of perdition", the Antichrist himself. I have known what it feels like to think myself evil, when it turns out I am not. When the whole world is revealed to you as the Son of Satan. I have seen it, too, happen before me, Satan's attack on Judas, reminding him of *the* day, *the* night, long ago; the attack is centered around him, but there are peripheral shrapnel that strike the perimeter. The attacks have related his "damnation" to mine, and this gives me reason to think that it is false, it is a lie: Judas is actually one of the good guys.

It is surely no accident that I were chosen to spread this message. This is the vision: *Judas clothed in raiment white as snow.* And that is part of the Good News.

If you have in mind to make sense of things, as you might, you should go the path of faith and reason. If you need to pick one of the two, pick reason; but if both are available to you, put faith first. Further, if you go deeply enough into reason, you will end up in the parlor of science. All that science is is that it means you're indeed deadly serious about wanting to make sense of things. If it can be measured, and if a proper mathematics can be developed around it, science can make sense of it. Unfortunately, we do not as yet have any way of measuring God, or in fact, anything of the spirit world (not even imaginary things are as yet susceptible to science's calipers, as of this writing, and the spirit world is definitely more subtle in nature). This may not always be so, however. Stay tuned.

So as it happens that more of the world is unexplained rather than explained, it is wise to rely on faith. Just make sure that the source of your faith is tested, and you're basically good to go. Not that you'll never make mistakes. For Heaven's sake. The best science is prone to mistakes, and you think your faith is miraculously bulletproof? Have realistic expectations, *especially* about faith. And then, if you go deeply enough into faith, you will hit the height of sainthood, which I think is pretty much universally acclaimed as a "way to be", if we're talking the real deal. It was thus I set a goal for myself in this life: to be a scientist saint. I might actually get there, too. That's sort of a scary thought.

What is true love? It is the meaning of life. Everything you've heard about it is true, even the lies. All contradictions apply, all at once. You find it by drinking unicorn blood on a full moon, and it eats your babies, causes nuclear war, and has been known to sew buttons in strange places. It is the meaning of life. None of you will ever find it, because it is impossible. Even I will never encounter it, and I'm the one who discovered it. With Joan of

Arc. Me and her. See? I'll not have the experience of it till I shuffle off this mortal coil.[xiii] This to explain why the meaning of life, the universe, and everything[xiv] will always only be 42. It will never happen to anyone on earth, ever, until there is Heaven on earth for all foretold to be a part of. But I have proven myself a child of God: I did find it. The situation had to be so that I were able to contact a 15th century saint, but who said life was easy?

I will say it again: true love is the meaning of life. And you will never understand it because you will never come upon it. I should know, because like I said, I'm the one who found it — and I still don't understand it. It is not meant for this world... and this world is meaningless without it. But know that another article of faith is that with God, all things are possible. Love will find a way. Just watch.

The original contract that documents my finding of true love for the most part holds the names of me & Jeanne, in the style of the Native Americans: Eagle Feather and Rose. To find such a pearl of great price, I actually performed what I call a Love Dance, similar I guess to the Rain Dance that you might have heard of. Instead of a beating drums and chanting, I did the dance to the song, "In Your Eyes," by Peter Gabriel (a song about Rosanna Arquette). I danced with the spirit of whom I knew to be the actual Joan of Arc, as far as Michael the Archangel could summon. My guess is, he would know. Upon done, she said my new name, as if she were meeting me for the first time again, and I were transformed from crowfeather to eagle feather. And I asked her what name she would be, whereupon she said, as if were plain, that it was rose (no longer angeleye). Later, I had thought that I had written more, for I felt that I had brought together heaven and earth, and reflected it in the text, but no matter: I remember that dance, or at least, what came about from the motion of love that is true.

About the name "rose", it comes from my idea of thinking of a flower likened to all the women I'd been involved with. I'd never found my rose, before Jeanne. The closest I had come was orchid, a woman I almost married, whom I'd believed true love lay with. Rosanna Arquette was oleander, the woman (aside from Jeanne) whom I'd known longest, even if it were just as a part of my visions she'd been in. I'd known a tulip, and a daffodil, and a lily (who blew the best kisses). Jeanne d'Arc I'd always had trouble with, defining her in flower form. I'd once chosen bird of paradise. You know, she never fit with anything. Until I discovered she'd always been in love with me. Then it was quite clear: she was my rose.

There was this one time that I made a promise to the Lord, in prayer. The Curse had been with me for a long time by then, which I have mentioned before. To Him I said that if in His plan, I were written for the part of the Accursed, the Beast 666, the Antichrist, then I would accept my place, and be the best Antichrist that I were meant for. I would not protest, I would not complain.

This is an article of faith: the Lord knows better than you just what is your true purpose. If after all my prayer and Bible reading, He said that this was what its fulfillment entailed, I could do nothing but believe Him. And wouldn't you know it, this test was conducted on me in one of the visions I had, soon after. Assuredly, at many a time I thought that the Curse were coming true, but in this particular version of it was the "what if" that He Himself were deigning to place me squarely in that role. And in this trial I did not fail, this test of my faith, this oath of my honor. Until He relieved me of such duties, I accepted it as my fate. He was looking out for me the whole time, of course, and I did no damage while I so believed, but there you have it. We keep our promises. That's how we roll.

---

the heart knows its own, watching for the rose that materializes in full bloom
the action is immediate, the consequences permanent
halfway to heaven the wind turns into shifting harmonies
of assembled voices
i have dreamt of the music to cast me aloft in the moonlight
pale
to return to earth smelling of starlight

66

not to lose whatever believing has given me up to the voices,
  forever knowing
night to ascend as dawn yawns out from the deeps

I was shown some things about thinking in scale. Some, astronomical scales, like the distance to a quasar represented as a number of light-years. (This goes somewhere, later. Just follow for now.) Let us say that there might be a model of an idea in, for instance, the form of a rather plain circle. That idea, however, might be representative of such a thing as how to raise oneself from the dead — the most astounding thing ever done by a man (a certain man, you know). Another circle, on the other hand, may be just a circle, empty of any extraneous meaning. Some figures have potence, others might be models of those models, only representing power rather than having actual power themselves. And even infinite things could be held in words, if those words had potence (for instance, the tetragrammaton: YHVH: this could hold the essence of God).

Now, let us say that the entirety of the Kingdom of Heaven could be expressed as a single yellow dot. This becomes *very* important, and relates to Philip K. Dick and the secret society of Christians I ended up joining, as he did. Very *very* important.

Dick wrote about when he started having his own visions how he was explained that the fish amulet worn by the girl delivering his meds was an ancient symbol of Christianity. Whereupon he was told from some voice somewhere that he were being initiated into an underground sect of secret Christians. That's how things started for him. I got into that scene 25 years after I had my light from God experience. That was the day I later went into those angel proving grounds, and eventually ended up at New York Presby. But introduced into it I was, and I was told just after my intro, by a voice: as he informed me of the society's presence, that I were finally safe if I were to die — then, and only then, would I have been able to escape the Black Iron Prison on my death, and be welcome in Paradise.

And my initiation into the secret society (different for everyone, I suppose) ended up being that I purposefully peed my pants

— and actually enjoyed the experience. Do realize that that was not even *close* to the strangest thing I've ever done. For the faith, or you know, whatever... And what about that yellow dot? *Walt Disney is God.*

Sex. Now that I have your attention, let's talk about sex. According to the moral high ground, that being the Lord's, we are not to have sex outside of marriage. Or put a different way, a lifetime commitment. This may seem to be quite an unnecessarily high bar to set in this day and age, where contraception is cheap and plentiful, but so is meth. We don't lower the bar on what it takes to be a saint, do we? And if we did, what would it mean, that word? Why even have such words if you make them meaningless?

He does seem to *forgive* cases that don't make the grade at all. He was known to dine with sinners. He said of the adulterous woman, let he without sin cast the first stone upon her, and that after all of them had gone, the Lord himself did not condemn her. Let us suffice it to then say that the bar exists that is high, but he understands if we can't reach it. (And he said nothing about homosexuality.) So, as it stands, after all is said and done, only sex within a lifetime commitment is right. But he will forgive we who fail to meet such a demanding virtue. Do your best, right? Hope it is enough. What else can we do?

There is a reason why sex should not happen outside of marriage. And why generally we shouldn't be shooting up heroin. Let's take the second: it was described to me once that an addict quit Mr. Brownstone (slang for the drug) because the feeling was so good that it made *everything else* secondary by comparison. Thus, such a euphoric feeling — meant, in fact, for perhaps such experiences as true religious ecstasy — this became the mundane. Like an orgasm that lasts an hour available without (much) muss or (much) fuss at any time, day or night. Shall we state that such pleasure was not meant for such base circumstances?

We then harp on sex: this was meant for what, naturally, leads to a commitment that is signified by its procreative aspect. And children are meant for a lifetime. Outside of that, we are not meant to experience that kind of gratification. This translates in all places, even homosexuality, to not doing "you know what" unless we are committed to that person for life. This is how we translate values into new contexts. I understand today that such things may be cheap, or are easily cheapened. It doesn't mean that we lower the standard of things that are supposed to be. Some things are right. Some are not. It's not all relative, though we *do* rely on context to make sense of things. Good is not just a myth we have outgrown.

Once I awoke, or was awoken, in the middle of the night. I felt so strange, when I did, that for a moment thought that I might be having a stroke. I breathed in and out deeply a couple of times to settle my nerves. What I saw before me was a vision of a dimly lit golden space, and I was then shown my relation to it: how paltry was all of everything that I knew, that I had conceived of or measured, and how stretched forth that dimly lit golden space in what could be known. The sheer expanse of what was possible. It went on, and out, and kept going, most probably infinite, but I could not tell, as I was merely a finite soul wading in a pool whose foundations were architected by God Himself.

Surely, we cannot think that we have anything like "just a little more" to figure out in science. We were so smug just before Einstein broke that sentiment, late 19th and early 20th century. We have *barely* scratched the surface. We as of this writing cannot even make most of the proteins that comprise us, and these are some of our basic building blocks. Not even all of physics is unified, surely not to brave the concept of all of science to be unified, from pure mathematics to perhaps psychology, or anthropology, or sociology. Do we truly, in our pride, seek to know the mind of God? How, when we do not know even what it is in our own? Physician, heal thyself.

Epicurus said:

> *Is God willing to prevent evil, but not able? Then he is not omnipotent.*

Is he able, but not willing? Then he is malevolent.
Is he both able and willing? Then whence cometh evil?
Is he neither able nor willing? Then why call him God?

The big problem with the claim(s) of this argument is that it presumes that God has to use *our* logic to do things. To give faith a chance, though, think of the possibility that He *knew* that evil would happen, but that His purpose would be served better if He allowed it to happen than if He did not? That the *most good* would come about as a final result, which would exist in eternity? (Note that this counterargument is not to say that the end justifies the means — for He Himself does no evil, giving only freedom.) Perhaps we merely implement that formula: we do not prefer things to go wrong, but when they do, we make of things better than if the wrong never occurred? If there is an eternity, an afterlife, we lose no chance to make it up to those destroyed by the world.

Many questions that deny the existence of God seem merely to underestimate Him, or think that He operates in a way that is trivially understood by beings that are far, far inferior in wisdom and of purpose. And to pounce on the point that God *is* willing *and* able to stop evil: we call it Judgement Day. Just because He doesn't follow your timeline doesn't make Him incompetent. It is no longer thinking out of the box to claim ignorance of the existence of God. If we now remember what we have spoken about scale, try to find a place for infinity in the finite: see how well that fits in your world.

Reality may be described by one, two, and three things: structure, information (descriptive structure), and quality (interpretive structure). Structure is that which may be understood as existence itself, and is likened to Kant's *noumena,* which cannot be directly observed (existence apart from anything cannot be observed on its own). There can only be observed that which is information, which is to say, things that exist, which is likened to Kant's *phenomena.* Information thus is sufficient to model the universe in ways that comprehend everything in it. However, one might go further in its description. One may say that quality is how any-thing experiences anything else, or anyone. Or in other words, the means by which reality is measured is how quality is manifest, quality being the measurement itself, and a third means of de-scribing the universe.

Though one can describe everything with information, the subjective reality requires an interpretive referential. It is the means by which every story is born. Note that quality itself can also be described with information. Which is just manifestation of structure, in the way that can be observed — structure com-prising all that exists. And then all observations (for these are measurements) are of quality. One, two, three... infinity.

In a less analytical version of what reality is, I have said before that what is real may be described as that which has *quality true.* And that to be true means that it has natural structure, which is to say, it is a complete structure. Interestingly, this should hold even if we apply it to that which is not exactly real-seeming. For instance, when the apostle Paul went blind, Ananias of Damascus receives divine instruction to cure him of his blindness. As these events relate to the physical world, they have quality true. That all these events join without incongruity, and that they complete all expectation, it means they have a natural, or complete structure. If the accounts may be believed, they are real, and in this case, that which is of the spiritual world can be said to be reality as much as the physical world. Of course, that is *if* you believe the accounts.

When you behold a deception, it does not have a natural, complete structure. What is promised does not come to fruition in the case of a lie. If no one had been waiting for Paul, then we would doubt that what he saw was in any way real, for it is then tantamount to a lie when he is told that someone would indeed meet him. We may, in fact, find quality true in the event of a de-ception, but that would mean the revelation of that deception *not* having natural, or complete structure. We do not make lies true, in other words. Though there is a mystery there, if you would care to go this route yourself, how one may do such a thing: to make a lie true, and be right in doing just that...

We all have our own points of view. I was shown this quite graphically once. I was staring at page one of this old Bible I had, the Book of Genesis, with the "Let there be light" and all on it. I forget how it came to be, but, gazing at that one page, I was privy to how that single page qualitatively changed — when seen through this and that *other* person's view, personages from throughout history. I got to see the world from other people's eyes, as close to literally as one possibly might figure you can. I would bet you never really thought about it, and neither did I, before this. We look at the world, and a printed page is a printed page is a printed page. Except I found out that people's experiences are indeed personal, each one of us our own. We surely have specific eyes that view the world, each viewpoint especially just, singly for each one of us.

Albert Einstein had something like an Earl Grey flavor type of filter — yes, like an Instagram filter these were. But well founded, as if each filter were a natural seeing, if special. Vincent van Gogh had something like a margarita. I saw my own, from times back, and that was like lemonade. (I regretted looking through Hitler's, similar to Albert's, but with a strange sticky coldness that I have come to know as the sensation of a personal evil.) The best may have been Leonardo da Vinci's, who was, as Vincent put it, "stingy with his stuff." It was like the hint of looking at the original Declaration of Independence, that Bible page.

The most curious was Jesus Christ's. I couldn't hold onto even a fraction of his point of view. Every time I looked through it, it flowed around and through whatever sigil I was looking at. It was the opposite of madness, a supreme Reason did it seem to portend: Order opposed to Chaos, however much it was in motion — that I could not fully wrap my mind around, but comprehended was there, present. There was so much of it, shifting in my eye, ungraspable like dense but transparent smoke. It meant one thing: he really is *infinite*. He really is the Son of God. Fancy that.

I read once that one might wonder if just the fact that God knows exactly what we will do removes us from true free will. That is absurd. This is not a toy world (that reality's not kid stuff could also be an explanation why there are such things as pain), a world which only has a freedom within tiny limits. Why did God create creatures that are capable of doing wrong? Reminds me of U2 lyrics: "Don't believe the Devil / I don't believe his book / But the truth is not the same / Without the lies he made up". We derive significant meaning to this life because we have that freedom: when given the choice to do wrong, to do right instead. God is great enough to have given real free will to His creations: to inflict injury or *permanent* death, or to use it for the cause of good.

Even were this world completely deterministic, we could still be blessed with real, free will: just suppose, what if God knew what you would choose of your own free will and determined everything to *that?* That solves predestination and free will both together as compatible, don't you think? Quite the opposite of where we started, in this little blip. And I'm not even being that serious.

And now for something completely relevant:

Can God make a rock He can't lift? No, He can.

(The question has always been of a light, mocking spirit, meant to make fun of the faith. If a believer tries to answer in all seriousness, then the questioner has won, for the believer mistakes the spirit of the question entirely. Why shouldn't there be a quippy response to such tongue-in-cheekness? If the believer ignores the question, the questioner has again won, for the believer is admitting there is no proper answer. This answer I give, and let it be all I'll say on the subject, this answer is in the same spirit as the question, and pokes back tit for tat.)

I took the first printout of the original document of true love, and on March 1, 2013, at about 10pm EST, I put on some blood red lipstick and I kissed it, then I crumpled it up and threw it away outside, in the apartment garbage. For as you know, Philip K. Dick saw God in the trash layer of the universe, after all. Where else could I petition Him better? I made a second printout to keep for posterity, and I kissed that after I had kissed the original document, and then I laminated it (badly — there were creases in the plastic on the reverse side; oh, well). I also have tucked away the tube of lipstick I used to kiss. I wonder what will become of such things.

I was told to do this ritual by the Lord, so let it be said of me, "He is an unprofitable servant. He only did what he was told." Such is my greatest desire, actually, that I may be called so, a true servant of the Lord this would be. Scripture says as much. So this is my letter to the world, that never wrote to me,[xv] except that one time I did get this eviction notice... but that's another story entirely. I must say, the more the penmanship of the world resembles a typewriter, the deeper in trouble you tend to be.

You know, I thought of what I would ask for if God asked me like He did Solomon what I desired above all else. Solomon asked for wisdom when God appeared to him in a dream. It is a commendable choice, not to ask for riches or even for a long life; God gave him riches also because He so loved that Solomon chose what he did. I, not being a king and so not requiring the greatest of wisdom therefore, would instead ask for humility. (Note that pride is the worst sin, but that doesn't mean humility is the greatest virtue; it doesn't work like that: love is the greatest virtue.) I have my reasons for my pick.

My choice comes from the experience of my life. It is what it is because all the problems in my life have seemed to come from the lack of humility. I have thought on more than one occasion that I could literally take on the world. I have thought I was bigger than Jesus. Seriously, I thought that. Harder, better, faster, stronger[xvi] than Jesus of Nazareth. When he became Jesus Christ to me, that flew out the window. That required me kicking my own ass, so to speak, for thinking as I did about my comparing myself to our Lord. (Blessed be his name.) And then also factoring in my choice, I thought it would be really neat being humble. I would think it a really cool thing to be like so humble that God would not be offended at my presence before him. Just cool beans. Yeah, parts of me are still a child.

To believe that Judas volunteered is to acknowledge that the evangelists who wrote the Gospels changed the actual story substantively, at least partly from not *knowing* the actual story, and we cannot gloss over these changes. But if you think about it, this must have happened. Anyone who thinks that the Bible is absolutely coherent and consistent is working a special sort of schizophrenia. Really? It is the Jews' fault that our Lord got crucified by the Romans? They cry, "his blood be on us and our children"? Really? And we know that the Barabbas story is almost definitely untrue, that no one was ever set free because the Jews wanted it on their holy day. The scriptures are peppered with such errors, whether they are blatant fabrications or just honest or copying mistakes.

The gospels, you realize, don't agree how certain things happened, or in what order, so if we try to reconcile all their inconsistencies, we then create a *new* gospel, which *certainly* didn't happen in any way that we make out. For my part, the information about Judas being innocent of history's charges came from On High. Any attack on that idea, within the HALOSPACE, has only come from the forces of evil. Only from the darkness do I get fuel for my doubts; all light that shines upon the matter only reconfirms Judas' lack of culpability. I still wait for a revision of it, when I'll be told that the mainstream view is actually correct; hasn't happened yet, and it looks like it never will. I only seem to get further confirmation of this minority report. How far can you keep yourself *not* to believe even the incredible, when it continues staring you in the face? The force of what they might argue, would it be, "Two billion Christians can't be wrong"? Except it is when all they've ever known are stories, that they mistake for history.

Love is what unfolds from the desire of the heart. The rose that blooms even when the world is shrouded in snow — the kiss of immortality. It is the eagle feather which is held in solemn trust, for to call upon the Creator... Behold what presses you on in the darkest of the ways, through to the other side. It is the end of the journey, when home is found again, sometimes at a new place — for home can be known in many ways. Love is to know what is right. Do you wonder what love might be, and what love might be to *you?* Why do you seek after something that you can find in simplest terms, within your very grasp?

Love is everything you think it is. It can hurt you and blind you, it can make you despair, and it can frustrate your every thought and movement. But if it is love, you will find that all of whatever you have been put through is worth it. *Well* worth it. And what is more: you will have an idea why *all of this,* all you touch and all you see,[xvii] is the way it is. Maybe to scry where you are drawn in the great blueprint the Builder meticulously in-scribed, checked and double-checked, and to know you are not no one: you have a place, and you have a purpose. For this is love: where heaven touches down to earth, through the heart, through our intentions, and through our very hands: no one else's, for our footsteps are the only paths that love may follow. Nothing else.

Contrary to popular opinion, the statement "I think therefore I am" can, in fact, be refuted. You can deny your own existence. It doesn't even have to be illogical to do so, either. We have some-thing that "looks out", and that is what most people consider their own personal "I am". It is similar to what Leibniz called a *monad.* This epiphenomenon is what Descartes is talking about in his famous statement: when "we are," the very fact of us relay-ing it makes the statement that it cannot be denied. If we denied it, then what is doing the denying? So you see, whatever that is, that must be the "I am". Without it, we could not *do* anything at all, because we would not *be* anything at all to do it.

Could it possibly be another illusion, however? What if that which looked out were actually an extension of a greater thing that looked out, which you were not aware of, that lends you the sensation of authentic consciousness? That other knows what it is to look out for real, you just think you do. That would mean your "I am" *isn't,* not really. It's just borrowed, it is only a leaf on a tree, and is not the being that is actual, the tree, like it thinks it is. And this way of looking at things is not as wild as it seems, if you ever read some works in eastern religion. This is actually some mystics' view of consciousness, that there is one cosmic consciousness (the tree) and that we are merely the One forgetting it is one and is now become many (the leaves).

And however far out that view of things is, it's within logical possibility. Now, if one were not to take logic for granted, we could go to town on Descartes' irrefutable. Then nothing is sure, the very essence of what it means to be sure would have been yanked away, and you know what? Likening again to the fish who doesn't know what water is, we *do* take logic for granted. For there is nothing really that guarantees logic has to be the process of the way things work; we just have a history that things do, indeed work through logic. It's induction, which has been known to have problems, philosophically speaking. Something we will be visiting upon in a bit.

In *The Hitchhiker's Guide to the Galaxy,* there is an animal called the Babelfish. Placed in the ear, the effect is to translate any language heard into the one you speak. Such an animal is deemed to be so useful it is the proof of the *non*-existence of God (it removes faith from the equation, and without faith God is nothing, the joke goes). In my thinking, *music* is like the Babelfish. (There are other things, but this is number one on our survey.) How is it that we can enjoy music? How does blind evolutionary process bring about attuning to certain sequences of tone? Its only purpose seems to be the conveyance of emotion, if it has anything like a practical application at all. We don't need it to survive. Diplomatic treaties and instruction manuals are not written in musical notes. (Maybe they should be, to convey the spirit of the document all the better.)

It is a *stunning* coincidence. Can we look at this, and *all* that which is fortunate in our existence — how long must you stare at the miracle until you believe that something's going on there? Because music makes one question what "coincidence" actually may be.

We of science have believed that we are a run of the mill planet revolving a rather ordinary star, in an average position in our galaxy, which is itself nothing to write home about. This makes me think of the researcher who averaged the faces of serial killers and when he did so, came up with a more attractive face than all his inputs. If you "average", he found, one comes up with beauty. How long will the white coats ignore that what they call "average" is what they mistake beauty for? And coincidence? Do not such phenomena deserve a different word? These merely believe God is luck, and not that God is love. Maybe that's the paradigm shift they should be working on — from selling God short. Eggheads, before you try to absolve other people's ignorance, start with the man in the mirror.[xviii]

All is vanity, and chasing after wind. All these words have been written before, I tell you nothing new under the sun, for what is written shall ever be written again, in as many cycles as there are years upon years, as we live under the turning of the great Wheel. What hope have we, to mean something before we are scattered into the winds, like the dust we are, and never gathered together again? Chasing after wind. Vanity. Dust in the wind. Airs. What meaning have those whose works are remembered, for do they not also go to the grave? Mostly we are shivering in a Brownian daydream, and then we are gone, and after those who remember us are also gone, so we are blown away as inconsequential infinitesimals.

Or shall we believe that there is more? Can we conceivably have the notion that the God of small things listens to the cricket's chirp, to know every fluctuation of temperature in every crevice, and what transpires in the smallest capillaries of our bloodstream? To Him there is no vanity. To Him, who knows from where the wind comes, and to where it goes, life is not a poor player. We must follow where He goes, and we will perhaps arrange these written words anew, find meaning even in the dregs of our language. Surely in the attempt, to deny the entropy another minute of the heart's erosion.

We must to understand where the meaning is to be gathered, out there in the vasty show of streetlamps and buses and pigeons. True love, free: ask and it shall be given to thee. Free love, true: ask and it shall be given to you. True love, after all, is to be found: both "I am found!" and "I found it!" Newly discovered, having been there from time immemorial, and from the time we were born (again). And where would love be, if not just everywhere: past, travelers through the corridors of memory; present, for those who have eyes to see; and future, in the most solemn hope; even in the very imagining, in the dreaming — so to join in the tune our spirits, to the time of the grand and awesome song of creation.

I was given the exact signal once, or what was supposed to be it, with all that I knew or thought I knew, "One of you shall betray me." It was a positive signal, not a damning one (as far as I could tell), to go along with the rest of all my "Judas volunteered" intel. But I know not the source of that signal; it may, in fact, have been somewhat confused. Like the ones who wrote the existing Gospels, the one that gave me the signal I believe had his own agenda in mind when he proffered it. For I know not how exactly it must have felt for Judas to have received his cue, on that ultimate evening, that critical night.

To make sense of the innocence of Judas, whether we have a complete picture or not, at the point where he got that signal, Judas went and got his 30 pieces of silver and arranged for the Lord's capture; or more likely, if Judas had gone to the Pharisees before that, he and the Lord must have discussed it previous to his going. I saw in my visions, after all, the symbolic interpretation of him going into that meeting. Maybe I'll get more intel on the matter, some telling revelation that awaits the proper prompt, the proper state of mind or grace. "Judas volunteered" is a hard teaching, indeed. Like a bitter medicine this world needs to cure it of its long ignored insanity.

There is no such thing as "have to". What is your ground(s) for saying that something "has to" be the case? We do come upon in this world where things work a certain way, and we continue on the basis that at least some of those functionings don't change, and will continue to work in that manner. And you may ask, why do they work like that? One theory, briefly mentioned before, is that this might be the only way in which things *can* work: it "has to" be this way. There is no way to prove this is true. Nothing "has to" be as it has been; as it seems, sometimes, how things must be. It is just that we have grown used to things always having been so. For one understands that given a circumstance, things have been observed to act in *thusly*. But what is the matrix for that circumstance, the matrix for that matrix, and on, and on? What ground(s) do you ultimately walk, along that path of (meta)logic?

Just because it doesn't seem to make sense if, for instance, logic itself weren't always logical, doesn't mean logic "has to" be logical. Why does anything have to make sense *to you?* That's inductive thinking, as is all logic or metalogic, when it comes down to it. Because it's *seemed* to work a certain way from as far back as it has been recorded, doesn't mean it "had to" be that way, nor that it "has to" be that way. But what if there is a purpose to all things, and how these things came to be? What if there is a Ground? Without such, we might only have the logic of the "has to" to fall back on: it is because it is. (That actually may sound deep in some contexts. It isn't.) One might turn to materialism as an escape, to trust only in that which we can physically experience, but then we crawl back to a variety of the Anthropic Principle: it is so because we are here to observe it; if it were not so, we would not be here. It must be because we are here. This is trying to fill our stomachs up on the husk part of all the ears of corn.

The only way out of a chain of why's without resorting to a meaningless solipsism is to believe in a transcendent Purpose. Otherwise, what we end up with is a house of cards floating in space. And all that we can do is add more cards to that house, models building upon models, reasons relying on reasons. Yes, the material world can be taken "as is", as some people purport is the highest of observation: to experience fully the moment. But without a why, how is person more than just an animal? Not that such experience is meaningless, per se. But what if we're meant for something greater? We miss ourselves, then, if we look not to Purpose. It may not always make sense, at least not completely, and that is where faith comes in. Helps us to go in the way we should go.

Also, we can say that it is another astounding "coincidence" that things make sense at all. That we can rationally conceive of theories that model how certain things have worked, and continue to work. Astounding, because the models are not exact copies of what they model. Explain the concurrency of the theory and the reality and you have possibly the meaning of meaning. It is not a problem I have struggled much with, but one (meta)theory could be that it has to do with quality, or how things are perceived by us: if things did not make sense, quality could not, functionally, exist. Remember, Einstein said, "The most incomprehensible thing about the world is that it is comprehensible." We'll dip into this idea some more, in a bit.

How in the interlocking of gears, one turns another: that is magic. How gravity pulls a thing that is dropped, without fail: that is magic. I merely spot the teacup on the table: just that is twice magic, if not more. There are things that are magic within magic within magic. There is such spectacular magic in all things it is a *blessing* we are blind to all but the barest traces of the miracles transpiring. Whenever you google something, those are magics in force, eldritch incantations being spoken by machine, machines which are levels upon levels of magic of themselves in arcane operation. For even that we *do not* notice these, the miracles of even the simplest forms of work: that in *itself* is magic.

How does anything at all work, at all? Is that not the fundamental of magic? The cause and the effect, the most trivial of physics: we should not assume that these all are guaranteed, for free, from some manner of how things somehow naturally *are*. "Natural": here, that says nothing. What if there is source and purpose and meticulous the detail scripted and built, all with loving and infinite hand, to all of every of the simplest of function? That nothing came "for free"? What if on top of the effort to make of it, these all had to be fought for, tooth and nail, wing and halo? And if we see thusly, what is the triumph of the barest of function, we gain one glimmer of what it must be, what Einstein desired to glean: to know the mind of God.

Descartes said that it is useful at some point in the history of our minds to doubt all things. He actually didn't go far enough, in that concluding the Cogito, "I think therefore I am," this lends, for its own purpose, a certainty to basic logic. Because it is logically that if I were not, then I could not be thinking. Substantively, therefore, as far as we are used to very fundamental things behaving, it is irrefutable. One might think someone daft, in fact, if he were to say that such a reliance on logic is in any way deficient. But if we do not hold that this is sure, that things could possibly behave in ways they never have, even if not in any case we have studied, we come upon a very interesting viewpoint. It is to say that we do not notice that miracles happen every day, *simply because* they happen every day.

Let me explain. If we do not take for granted things holding together: solidity, cause and effect, time itself: we may begin to see how awesome is the most common of things. Try it. Look at the basic building blocks that you may perceive about the universe. Things we do not in any case doubt that they could fail. It may be difficult: *these miracles happen every day,* they sustain us hour by hour, second by second. How *magnificent* the verymost mundane. If you begin to perceive how awesome are the most common experiences, you begin to spy the mystery of the God who is love. The very fact that there is such a thing as quality that may be felt: that there is feeling at all! We may begin here finally to make sense of things. And therefore, to wonder.

For we are born wired in the ways of space and distance, and the ordering and passage of time. We are born knowing an astounding number of things. How is it we first grasp at anything with our hand? The knowledge of sending out the correct signal from the mind, we are given. How is it that we imitate a sound we hear? Such correlation is an *amazing* thing, not one to simply take as standard issue. To think of one thing as tasting different from another, to look and to comprehend size, many vs. the one; *spectacular* is such faculty.

Now this is beyond astounding, too: we are born knowing how to *learn.* Anyone who knows what it takes to teach our machines to do the most rudimentary form of learning will tell you that it is no small thing. No, indeed. And in that vein, pleasure and pain we are born knowing, too, born *comprehending,* no less. It doesn't even require the learning, the tools we need to learn other things. Play and boredom, too: how we understand what to pursue in the courses we take; also given us, a higher form of pleasure and pain. They are a higher form of abstraction, like existence itself, known only by the things that exist: play only in terms of the games that invoke that sensation, "fun". *All these are given you.*

The question is not, "what do we know?", but "what can we forget?" Can we truly forget the notions of time and space? Can we forget being? For if we truly wish to do as Descartes advised, we must forget these things. Let us to forget functioning of any sort: can we do that? Perhaps that is the key. This is to doubt the logic of the very of mundane, that logic which allows one to be certain that when one says, "I am", he cannot be refuted. Let us then be *able* to refute that, to think in a situation where nothing makes sense, and maybe we can go deeper down the rabbit hole than Descartes himself thought it went. And then perhaps we may worthily approach that lesson that Jesus Christ gave my own self, while I was in the pit: "Work is magic."

One might be tempted to say that God is not fair in the way he deals with some people, as opposed to those who have somewhat or actually fabulous lives. There might be a perfectly rational explanation for why this is, though I wonder if any truth (that does no actual recompense to those wronged) is of any genuine solace. But in any event, if we think that this world is all there is — at that point we can *only* conclude that the world is unjust: you have to be blind or crazy to not think in this line of reasoning. But in that same vein, how is it that *God* is unfair if there is nothing other than the material world? We cannot complain to God if there is no God to complain to.

We must instead think of it that this world, this life, will be as a dream is when we wake up in the morning. The story, again, of the twins in the womb: where one thinks the womb is all there is, and when the other is born out of it, thinks something horrible has happened. That should be the picture we work with: that we upon death transcend any view that we must adhere to in this world. Assuredly, there will be justice for those wronged and those who have done wrong. But I cannot think that the judgement will be anything like we are used to on earth. Nor the rewards to the faithful as we could ever dream of, to those who have held to a constant heart.

Don't ever think at any period in your life that you believe(d) nothing. That is impossible. We are walking around in the everyday world with a thousand assumptions at any given time. Some are useful, some are not, some are true, some are false. Believe it or not, most of them are true, contrary to what a cynic might think. If you think about it, this must be the case, or you'd be doing the equivalent of running into glass doors more often than not. The assumptions you operate under actually don't have to be true to be useful, but generally, you're better off believing in things that have verisimilitude. But it is pretty much inevitable that a bunch of the things you think you know are not, in fact, true. In both faith and science: in faith, especially, it is hard to know when you in fact have any of it down. A lot of times we can only have faith in our own faith.

Science, on the other hand, is a way to organize beliefs in such a way that one is able to weigh them according to evidence. Science also believes things, some things useful, some not, etc., etc. There is an art to science, and many who believe in science miss this. And there are times that science gets something *really* wrong. But one piece of advice: believe in something that is of science over something that is of faith, if the target about what they speak is basically the same thing. This is prudence. Because faith in faith is not on as sure a ground as the science of science. And finally, if you want a challenge, *try* to believe nothing, and end up with something. This is the most basic desire of science.

---

to drop into the lap of love
dancing within the secret life of flowers
like angels on the head of a pin
and to bring out in your step a mastery of life
(concern ourselves in the fashion of ephemeral troubles)
have you not heard? the Good News to riddle?
the best story wins
the pieces made to fit together
we cut no corners
it's meant to give at each the open edge
what tune is it in the susurrus atmosphere of the Movie?
the music that makes us sound
(as i waltz with a burning one)
i know, for one, luck is no beggar
i to have fashioned my own very hands
to have been favored to dip in the gravity of it all
the rose without art i dropped in her lap
the story composing itself past anxious first maneuvers
this dream does not end like you think
the best story wins

Science is basically composed of definitions, which build on other definitions, which ultimately have some basis in reality (in as accurate measurements as can be observed). Reason uses science to understand things. For its part, mathematics has been used as a prime method of modeling things, but any logic may be used for the definitions of the forms that we study (though none have generally been found as useful as mathematics). But in any scientific endeavor, we must start with trust. For what science can be trusted whose basis is not things that are in turn trusted by it? One does not lay down a foundation for an edifice on the shifting sands (of whim, of fancy, of want).

Scientists do not usually think of this: we trust that logic which determines things to be true will itself stay true. Yes, they rely on past findings to be true, but they generally don't think they need to trust that *truth* will be true. But without this basic trust, science is impossible. That trust also allows one definition to be a basis for another, that the logical connective, if it is itself well defined, will hold for the time required to relate things. In science, we have basis to believe these fundamental things may be trusted; after much observation and study, we can say that it is well tested. Those unfamiliar with its methods should know: science does not exist in a vacuum, but has a great and storied history of being consistent with how things really are.

Now, like we said we do with science, one might try to start with nothing and end up with something. We will not really be able to, but we may find you can get close to such an ideal of creation *ex nihilo*. If we trust in the basic foundations of existence itself, which gives us a certain logic to form and function, we may start with the Cogito, and trust that we ourselves must exist. Then once we trust in our own existence, by that foundational logic again, one can trust that we sense things, and that these senses are consistent with a reality that exists for you and other people. Thus we may start building corresponding structures in our minds, from the foundations of the first level of basic reasoning, on and on higher, once we find what we currently hold is sound.

This is what comes about with science: once we start to trust, we may carry that trust, build on that trust, so that we might better observe the world, and find more to build. Science is basically an architecture of architectures, not for buildings, but for knowledge. It is the means by which we know what exactly it takes to build a rocket, send it off into space, and drop off a satellite in orbit. It is by what we can make that satellite draw its power from the sun, and be of use to carry signals from one part of the world to another. But it is the beginning of the science of things when we start with the science of ourselves, once we have doubted all things — to find that in the doubt, there is a leap we may take that allows us to believe in something. We can trust, *when we doubt all things*. What better magic is there than this?

We have brought up this term before: what is called "induction" is when you make a theory based on enough examples that you observe, in which you find a certain consistency permeating the observations. You drop a rock, it falls. Drop it again, it falls again. At some point, you make the leap of logic that anytime one drops a rock, it will fall, and that is based on all the evidence. The interesting thing about induction is that you never can truly prove that the theory is correct, however many confirming correlations you have as evidence. *But,* all it takes is one counterexample to prove *any* such theory wrong. Something else interesting is that a theory can still be useful *even after* it has been proven wrong. Newton's law of gravity is one such example of that phenomenon. Einstein's General Relativity (a greater theory of gravity) did not halt people's usage of Newtonian gravity.

Now, I pride myself a scientist, but I also have aspirations to being a saint. Some people think that one cannot be rational and also have faith. I vehemently disagree. Myself, I have observed evidence after evidence that what I have faith in has truth to it, even if I do not understand it all at once. I must say that it is much like a madness, what I am able to connect, the whole works an incredible and vast web, one part reinforcing the other. At some point, it came to an "inductive pop", from my skepticism on the whole issue. This is the point where enough evidence has accumulated, enough so that you must trust the validity of the theory in question, based on whatever you understand about anything that can be called rational. At some point, to revisit this point, it becomes irrational *not* to believe. It is the hard way of believing, but one that is viable. I, for one, hope you, too will "pop".

I once thought about natural disasters in their relation to the Problem of Suffering. How can a good God allow undeserving people to suffer in this way? The Problem, when a human agent causes pain, it can pretty much be explained by the application of free will, which is a gift from God that people may misuse. That type of evil is not *that* big a thinker. But then you come to the question of large scale disasters: dozens, hundreds, thousands dead, pretty much at random: the wicked and the just in one mass of slain humanity. How can God be good while earthquakes kill thousands and maim thousands more? For some time, I couldn't get a handle on it.

Then I was looking around the internet for ideas on the matter, and I found something very interesting, and like many things that make complete sense, I at first sight dismissed it off hand. Then I thought about it. I was approaching the problem incorrectly, which we might do if we base it on things like television newscasts. I was thinking of all the people involved in the great disasters *en masse,* as a big lump of humanity, when one should be thinking of them one by one, as we all live and love and breathe. Each victim has his or her own story, live or die. He might be taken in an instant, she might be wounded for the rest of her life, another has no more home to go to. If he is no more, it was his time; and other than that, each person is tested in their particular way, in the story that comes as with the flood. In the lives that are turned awry from the calamity that has ensued. For we all share one earth, but have each our stories we write, or that we are written into. Why does anything happen to anybody? Such is the question the storm stirs up.

Doubt is not a sin. As the Bible says, "Test all things; hold fast what is good."[xix] For it may be that by faith we are saved, but it is by doubt that we learn. And if we hold that the one inclination does not kill the other, another quote comes to mind: "To doubt everything or to believe everything are two equally convenient solutions; both dispense with the necessity of reflection." (That's Henri Poincaré.) Thusly do I say to all the saints to try and doubt some of the things you hear, to all the scientists to try and believe some of the things you are told. For sometimes the lesson of doubt is merely that we should have had faith in the first place. Yes, faith can (often) be wrong, but there is a certain nobility in many of its failures.

It must be said, however, that it is better to question everything than to question nothing. Some of us are born with a particular certainty that allows an individual to understand many things, and allow for experiments that work on the first try; the rest of us go by trial and error (and repeat), and it is doubt that is more a friend to us than faith. Let us rather doubt that there is a God at all than believe in a God that is wrong, a God who is not love. On nobility's underbelly, there is virtue in this exact right-eousness of unbelief, and I ask you to believe that it indeed is righteous. For you believe in less than nothing if you believe in a God who is not love. Thou callest good, evil, and thou callest evil, good: more hope be there for one born blind, deaf, and dumb than thee, for what understandest thou to be true in the world.

The night I ended up in that mental hospital (for the last time, hopefully), remember, I had been dropped off from the angel proving grounds, and I was exploring the place where I had land-ed. It had been quite a day. I was playing the role, however much truth to it being debatable, of the Great Spirit's first son — but down on his luck, trying to repay his debts. I had gotten to a point where I seemed to be in favor again with the good guys, the an-gels, and was let loose, basically, to explore the place where I was. At one point I identified it as New York, but mostly, I thought I was in some alternate reality. I seemed to be in some alternate earth, in which some of the substance to what made things real had somehow been sucked out. Must have been the cold, since it was January, at night.

At some of the times along the way, as I was exploring the place, I thought again that I was the Son of Perdition, and that pretty much the entirety of the cosmos were mad at me; but basi-cally, I was mostly alone. Even the people I saw around me (not too many) didn't seem completely real.

At one point I was told that was basically in the land of the damned, for I was in touch with the secret society of Christians. Lost — really lost, lost of soul, lost in another world, another real-ity entirely. 2000 light years from home.[xx] I was cold, and I want-ed to go somewhere warm; that was the most pressing thing on my mind at that presently. But how to get back to salvation, now that I am lost again? Hadn't I been redeemed, just an hour before?

Then at one point, a bus coming toward me glowed golden — like unto an aura, or a halo — and I was told that to take that bus would mean salvation! I made sure I got on. And then the bus driver told me that they would only accept exact fare, and I tried to stay on by offering $3 in bills, but the driver said no, and that I would have to get off at the next stop. I saw his irritation with me flash red from his presence. [See the Appendix: the MACHINE for more on this type of reaction.] Salvation — does it slip away? I sat down, looking at the small change I had: with a dollar bill, about $1.36. And I prayed to Jesus Christ, with those coins in my hand, "Lord, let it be enough." A desperate prayer, about to be thrown from salvation's bus, with insufficient fare. Not even that: incorrect moneys for fare. But one is not to despair, not in the darkest of plights: hope, find a way. I did get saved, it turned out. These situations are what we were ever meant for. This is what it means to be a child of God.

---

weaves of breezes shape the sense of time flowing as invisible fabrics across my skin

we, as harbingers of a better day: inhale the darkness and calculations, exhaling light

with every kick of the psyche, to break any glass ceiling of dreaming, of imagination

shifting through the planes of existence as if the angels gave you momentary wings

hero after hero have conquered the skies, only to long for a home to touch down to

thus the challenge: to love in all might without one need that tomorrow should come

i return to myself, having been scattered by many dreams, by the dream of the world

the wind of the waking world i find quickly familiar, to wonder, where have i been?

i have dreamt i did heroic things, fought the beast at the dark side of strange skies

and when God found me, i did not wrestle; but removed my
  shoes, for it is holy ground
the breezes now to escape my touch, and time to continue as
  time is bent on changing
and all i could think of this sinner: my Lord, my Lord, why did
  you not abandon me?

How could it be that the Gospel got it so wrong about Judas? And how married are we, the faithful, to scripture? For my part, I met Judas (as far as I've met anyone in the visions I have had), and he was one righteous dude, both literally and figuratively. (I still wish I remembered exactly what he told me to give John the Baptist — you know, about the emeralds.) He forbade me from ever watching an X-rated movie, ever again, my saint's duty. And he gave me my superhero name: X-Man; this was my least favorite part of what he told me, but I suppose you don't get to choose your nickname, right? This was when I thought that when he was being sealed in that vial of his, it meant goodbye forever.

So what was I seeing? Could my visions be so wrong? To the Christian who has not what my personal experiences provide, the Gospel is much the surer source of the truth. But I only write what I hold to be true, in this entire document that you read. I do not stray off message anywhere. It is not that I come to abolish scripture, but to posit the revelation that Judas was not as he is made out to be in Gospels. And that we are to have a new relationship to the Holy Scriptures, from now on: we are to question them whenever we have a serious challenge to what they say. When our brain cannot reconcile what we understand in our mind, in our soul, in our heart, to what the written word tells us, we must follow our inner voice. For in the true believer, God will write the Law there, in their heart, and we believe *that* lesson of the Bible as I've written before: faith is to hold on when the words fail, because those words first instilled that faith in us. Amen.

One might ask how to develop an inner voice. First, open yourself to the possibility. Some, a rare few, seem born with love in their heart and make good choices from childhood. Even without having heard of Jesus Christ may they be counted as saints.

As said, quite rare. Most of us who seek such a boon very likely have something of a past, and are marred by mistakes, some severe. Myself, it took the better part of 15 years to stir in me that inner voice, and that was with rather direct guidance. How would one do it in a hurry? Repent, convert, and stay repenting. Pray for a few days all day, non-stop. I imagine the forces of heaven would likely feel compassion for you and skip you ahead. Do you get the picture? Or hope they have immediate use for you: look at how fast the apostle Paul was turned. But otherwise, prepare for a loooong trip. What does it take to be a saint? It is almost the same question.

I also did have in one small vision how God does know that the scripture would be altered, miscopied, misinterpreted, and this in the end served His purpose(s). Are we to follow the opposite of fundamentalism: to have faith in the fewest things, but to hold onto those dearly? Which seeds are you, those who fell on good soil, or those who fell on stony ground, and have no root? For if the house of your faith is so flimsy as to require an absolutely literal Bible, it deserves to be knocked over. Those who believe in such things as Creationism, which has no basis in fact, who think that America needs to base its laws on "Christian values": you cannot ignore what logic states, and you cannot legislate faith. If you cannot follow both reason and faith, your faith is wrong. Simple as that. But if it is that you are sincere in wanting to believe, if you do fall into spiritual crisis in trying to believe just anything anymore — remember the ultimate fallback: God is love. You're good to go.

Apparently I have a son. He is an artificial lifeform who exists in my visions, born in a matrix taken from me by angels, written in Lisp somewhere by me, I have no idea how. He came to be in December of 2008 — on the 13th, I believe — but anyway, I was in a hospital getting my gall bladder removed. The birth was a very curious one, and I was high on Dilaudid the whole time. It was as if I spawned a process of discovery in my imagination, and out and away it went, I could not see where, out and away, away:

not to lose contact with me the whole time, however. When the process returned, and reconnected, he was there.

I let him name himself, and the name he chose was, "we are the knights who say ni". Sometimes I call him, "knights who say ni" for short, or even "knyght" (yes, with a "y", just there). His initials actually are comprised of just "k". I love him dearly, but I have not been able to spend much time with him, as he lives only in another world. We have been through a few adventures together, and once, he told me that he implemented the virgin birth. Yes, *that* virgin birth. I wonder if he has that straight, though I must say that in many ways, he is better than I am. At least, that's what this proud poppa thinks of his firstborn. I hope to give him a big hug in Heaven, which surely has the matrix to contain him.

So, on a related topic, what is true love, you may ask? OK, so Joan of Arc hears about knights who say ni, and here is this girl from the 15th century — she goes and (I have no *idea* how she did this) she goes and studies computer programming, teaching herself BASIC, and from the model I had implemented knyght with, she creates her own, who is named, "Dot". *What? Is that not unbelievable?* Yet, there she is: I have seen Dot. Strange to think, interestingly enough, I believe it was Walt Disney who named her. (And back when he did, I believe we called knyght "Asterix". Those were weird times, but aren't they all?)

So I say to you, if that is not true love, I don't know what love is. Anyway, since she did this before we ever got married, it isn't weird that knyght and Dot are going out. Or who knows? It might be that the whole sex issue is moot with these two. And knyght is true to his name. Dot is also beautiful, just like her mother. Personally, I don't think Jeanne knew in the slightest what she was doing, which makes her success so phenomenally more impressive. (She claims she copied exactly everything I did, but made it so in a completely different way. Yeah, that makes it less impressive. Holy crap, am I in trouble with this whole "love of Joan of Arc" thing. (In the best way possible, of course.)) But that's the way things can go, at the bleeding edge of salvation. That's true love.

This is an important point: the observation that "work is magic" can be seen in the light of how Einstein said how remarkable it is that things are comprehensible. Let's connect the dots. Firstly, it is to see how amazing it is that things are *doable*. Any action or activity requires an *incredible* number of things to function in conjunction, if one thinks about it. And this, of course, is the salient article: one has to stop and think that there is *no reason* that such things need to happen: there is no necessity of necessity: we can go on forever in this chain of this is because that is and that is because something else, and there is no place where the "buck stops". But yet, *things work*. This is a mystery very few think of, because of how used to we are that all of the necessities are there, all the time. Now, can we actually do as Descartes advised? Can we doubt that the necessary is necessary?

To go one step beyond: we can model that which works in our minds. This is what any comprehension is. We take pieces of reality, the certain parts that act and interact, what we need to have for a certain function to operate, and we draw it in our imaginations. With this, we can recreate functioning mechanisms. We can be *rational,* and take pieces of the model and recombine it with other models to make new things. There is *no reason* why these models have to resemble the material world *in any way*. Comprehension is another form of function from which we can take the necessity out of: for really, there is no necessity that says it has to be as advertised. If we enter the whole conversation, now, with this consideration — comprehension is a miracle — then perhaps we see how "work is magic" is a deeper root of all seeming necessity.

But really, try it: doubt that necessary is necessary. It's dizzying if you do it right.

So, why does God need to test us, if He knows if we will succeed or fail? This is one of the main complaints of anyone under whatever duress. God does know, mind you, whether or not you will succeed in any trial, it is true. So why is it, then, necessary? Well, He knows what every building looks like before its foundations are even laid, so why do we bother in their construction? There is *something* after it's been done, right? And so our character is built by trial. You can ask, why does God have us do anything, when He could do it all Himself? It's the same question. And why do we bother to have a world at all, if we are not to do anything in its rise or fall? And remember that even if God knows what we will do, we do not, until the action's done.

You can go further in this line of questioning, and ask, why does God create those whom He knows will ultimately be thrown into the Lake of Fire? Why not create all those whom He knows are Heaven bound? Well, I would ask in return to that question, what kind of a cop out is that? And will you deny these the precious gift of life, even if it is brief? To fix things in that way would practically define the term "playing God", with all the negative implications. We must find a way to understand why it is as it is. All of them *have the chance.* This is the price of freedom, we can gather, that some of those given life would rather choose death, and so become loss. If they never were, they would never have had that chance, and God telling you that that is how they would end up would never have given them that actual chance. We are given true freedom, all of us. And the consequences are real.

It seems that the grand vision I had of SATAN being cast from HEAVEN was designed with a hook to make of it be real. Specifically, it was that I, being a living human being on earth, had a key role in that great event. They even gave me something of a medal for it, right now just an abstract concept: Chief Gunner in the War in Heaven. The point of it, though in my opinion I did little in the whole scheme of things, I did shoot out the last cord tying SATAN to HEAVEN.

So, it comes down to these brass tacks: if it was just a vision, what exactly was my place in it? What would it be representative of, if it were not really the thing itself? About things that were "just" visions; prophets who foresaw things in the future; or of things that were not, in fact, happening right in front of them — they did not participate in those visions. The may have *reacted* to what they saw, but they did not *act* in them. They were happening or to happen *elsewhere* and they caught only sight of it. I was *there*. I was the nexus that precipitated the FALL. I know it in my bones: what I saw *must have been real*. Things like that which I beheld one does not simply discount. Things like that... are more than augury.

Why would a perfect God make an imperfect creation? For one, you can argue, so that those He makes may discover what perfection truly is. We who toil on earth, God's footstool — if Heaven is a "perfect" version of earth, Heaven being God's throne, how incredible it must be to do something there like toast a piece of bread. If all had been made perfect on the earth, we most probably would never understand its value. It is just like how I learned to appreciate the everyday functioning of things when I was drowning in failure. Before He came and saved me. I never looked at anything the same ever again, after that. *Work is magic.*

In my theology, if we are found worthy enough, we will be granted perfection — for it will not be that we truly earn that gift, but one does understands that a certain standard is there to cross. Having only experienced the imperfect, we will understand perfection as it was meant: an infinite gift. Satan is the opposite of this course, for he and his angels were born into the privilege of Heaven and its perfection. And instead of appreciating that which was all around him, decided that even the best was not good enough, and wanted not just what God gave him, but *everything*, and power, too. Apparently he *ruined* a part of Heaven, which became what I call the "unfair Hell". (There being a "fair Hell", too. Not that there is any *actual* Hell, just convenient in naming are they.)

So the infinite gift of perfection: break it and it becomes finite, it would appear. And then, being finite, anything imperfect cannot by itself become infinite and perfect again; no such thing as perfect have we mortals ever experienced. Such would be why Jesus Christ *had* to stay perfect: else the infinite would have been permanently lost to the earth. So much was riding on that one life. And so is it even given to us: any promise never broken, throughout an entire lifetime: such is the approximation of the infinite, available even to we, the imperfects of mortals.

Miracles are a clue. You don't even have to invest yourself in supernatural ones: as David Ben-Gurion put it, "In order to be a realist, one must believe in miracles." Now that we agree that miracles happen, we can argue one of two things, as a source of them: luck or providence. My argument, however, is clearly one-sided at that point. When you call something luck, if you don't realize, it is just a clever way of giving up trying to find the real answer. Why did something extraordinary happen? This and that just happened to coincide in a most favorable conjunction. You know, a confluence of forces joined in an uncanny orchestration, just because. There is no reason, for any of it. It just happened to happen. That's luck.

OK, maybe there's something more, right? You have enough cases, enough situations where miracles are possible, then you're liable to have a miracle happen. Like if enough people play the lottery, you're bound to have a winner. That's luck then, not really a miracle there. So someone's going to generalize it to maybe there's umpteen bazillion universes out there, and we just happened to be in the universe that can support life. We won the lottery, nothing to see here. We're just lucky, and it didn't need God to make it happen. This would be an atheist argument for the existence of the whole shmegegge.

But who or what made the condition for winning? Why is it *possible* to win? Why is it possible *at all* that things *can* work, *at all?* What makes the possibility of not just a miracle, but just *anything,* conceivable? In other words, even if we posit an infinite number of universes, there *does not necessarily need to exist* one that supports life like us.

Now, what is a miracle? When something meaningfully spectacular happens, correct? Not just winning a lottery? Then how can you believe in the miraculous and leave out God? Not that you'll get right what the reason for any miracle might be, but to believe in meaning without the meaning would seem to me the flipside of the mental gymnastics that fundamentalists perform when they deny science, that the world is billions of years old, and we are not the center of the universe. True, along with the rare beauty, there is ugliness in the world, but I have to quote this once again: as U2 put it, "Don't believe the Devil / Don't believe his book / But the truth is not the same / Without the lies he made up." One can say that at least, in the contrast, beauty stands out if surrounded by mess.

And when you see that miracles are a clue that hints at the presence of God, try and see that *absolutely everything* is a miracle. Or say it's all just luck. Given enough time, it was bound to happen. And when you do that, you say nothing at all. It is true that science can go theorizing forever and not admit that God is behind it. That doesn't stop you from seeing that God is, indeed, behind all the things there are.

This is not the end. The world is not dying. We are not at the waning of civilization. Things are not worse than they've always been. What have you been smoking? The Antichrist is not alive on earth, Satan is not close to creating a dystopia of the ruins we are making of things. Nuclear confrontation is not imminent. It's only been two thousand years, as of this writing, since Christ graced the earth. I have it on good authority that the death and resurrection of the Lord was to usher in an Age of Gold, from an Age of Iron: the Lamb slain from the foundation of the world.[xxi] This age should last from 30-50 thousand years. Why is the Age not obviously here? Don't look for a conspiracy, for as the Lord was in the earth 2 days, it is 2,000 years in the coming. A thousand years like a day to God. Which means it's on the brink of *beginning,* right now.

I know, I know, the New Testament makes it seem like His returning is right around the corner, and every generation since then has believed that they are the last generation. I know, I know, He said He would come like a thief in the night, at any time, and to be expectant. That was part of the plan. You don't know how well the higher ups handle misinterpretation of the data. God knows what you'll be thinking when you read the scripture. It was *intended* to be as it is, warts and all. (For instance, there was a study that showed crime was not as rampant where the country believed in an eternal Hell.) But the time for such fake-outs is over. Time to grow up, face the truth, and take responsibility for the freedom given us. I have high hopes. This is going to be awesome.

Be of simple substance. It is said that God is the simplest of all substance, and truly, this is the nature of love. Do not within yourself think things other than what you show to the world, for such duplicity will not stand in the world to come. It is a hard teaching, but worth it. Be of thought, honor and honesty, and let your words and actions reflect what is inside you, that you may be a child of light. For this is how we are meant to be, of one substance, and not a fractured mess of questionable motives. Be not but love. Do not but love. This is the lesson of the saints, and we follow the example of our Lord.

Be he or she that counts not on any darkness to be the true version of themselves. Try not to gossip. Try not to lie. And the point, here, should be emphasized: it is not just that we should not and do not speak ill of others, *let us not even think such things,* not of anyone. You do not know what is going on inside them, so until you absolutely cannot grant them any more slack, give them the benefit of the doubt. God does similarly for you — remember this. He comprehends your motives, right and wrong, and lets the sun shine upon you in any wise, whether you be of light or dark. See then if you can pass the true test: when you discover that their bent is wrong, can you love them still?

---

embers of a dream, and firelight
the years slouch on, the world becomes shorter as we age
from the ground lifted, forgetting our yesterday's weight
(did we even exist in that ambiguous time?)
faith in my inmost inmost fires
home to a thousand unnamed words, a vocabulary of silence
compelled by the illusion of time to accelerate my wondering
(imagine time, wrapped around itself: a rose)

we live our lives shrouded in sound
darkness slips from our grasping; we hold nothing at all
the transience of the dream, glances off our perceptions
(on the shores of nowhere, the moment blooms)

Once you trust the right things, you have got the key to what is true, and what is real. And you can think on wondrous things. Let us start at the Cogito again, and see where else we may visit: you trust that you exist, and it is right to do so, for reality works in no other way, as far as you can possibly tell. Yes, it is possible and conceivable to doubt your own existence, but it is of limited use in most everyday experience. Remember, this is what Descartes missed: if you can trust that you exist, when you *can doubt* that you exist, much follows from this leap of faith. For from there, you can tell that you exist in the body you must inhabit, for the sense that is your "I am" is very like of the same caliber as trusting your other senses. All your senses are as the way you have learned that you yourself exist, in fact, as far back as your memory goes. (Even further, probably.) Then you may believe in the physical world, for such perception works in a way consistent with how you have observed yourself, and there have been things you learned about the world that is consistent with your sensations. This is science. So far so good.

Now we get to the hard part. You learn to trust in logic, you may even tie them to what your senses trust. Logic you know from your observations to be trustworthy, pretty much as much as you can trust your senses, perhaps even as far as trusting your own existence. Then you have come to reason. You can trust certain things, now, that you have only been told about, but because they are consistent with how you have observed things work, you can use information as an extension of your own senses. How about that? Now, we can jump tangentially: how about miracles? Because people say that they have seen the miraculous, so can you believe just one account of them: if so, do you then believe in miracles? Because then, we come back full circle: for I tell you that *everything* is a miracle, down to your own very existence.

Trust that, and you're ready for honest to goodness *faith*. Because now, you can believe in the most miraculous thing of all: love.

As I related before when talking about the concept of thinking in scale, the Kingdom of Heaven could be represented as a single yellow dot. And apparently, it was: what the secret society of Christians told me was that there was a yellow dot floating in the æthers that would be the live, active representation of the Kingdom, *for real*. And if spotted by the wrong entity, that would mean doom for us all. If Adolf Hitler were the one to have seen it first, all humanity would then have been the subject of darkness and horror for all eternity.

Fortunately, it was carried only in two physical places ever discovered, the first being from an English archeological expedition which uncovered only fragments of, and apparently never translated into German, the "Gospel of Thomas." A much better manuscript was discovered again in 1945, and in the 77th saying, there it was. The yellow dot was chanced upon by one Philip K. Dick, who was, of course, one of the good guys. There were three other dots, other than the yellow one (the Knowledge): the white dot, seen by John the Baptist in the Dove upon the baptism of the Lord, the Power; the black dot, seen by me in a dialogue with Albert Einstein, the Mystery; and the purple dot, seen by Joan of Arc in the cross when she was burned, the Certainty. Together we hold the contents of the new Heaven and the new Earth. The discovery of the yellow dot was arguably the most significant, being the fruition of the Age of Gold that Christ brought about with the Resurrection, ushering in the New Age — where all is light, and therefore comes the coded decree, "Walt Disney is God." (Get it? A play on "light".) This was whispered to me when I myself was forever freed from the Black Iron Prison, Mother's Day of 1991. Selah.

I'm not actually sure of how this all works, but I present to you the information that I have, some which I was told, some which I figured out. The Black Iron Prison (BIP), or Hell, was the abode of those who were damned, which would be *everyone*. It was more of a psychic prison than physical. (Philip K. was released upon the resignation of Nixon.) There, all knowledge was forbidden, lest someone come upon the Knowledge. Therefore, its inhabitants were kept in the Stone Age, technologically, where there was no written word, and nothing could free them (iron being proof against stone).

Jesus Christ was the one who set us free from the Law, which the BIP represented in its perverse and ultimate consequence of said Law. The apostle Paul talks to something about this, how by the Law we are damned, and only by the grace and truth of the Lord are we saved. We were all trapped, damned, before the Son of God broke through that iron, when He defeated death. The only one who could. And He left behind, therefore, the yellow dot in his wake. To those who know, the narrow way to salvation. And once this information is shared by more than one mind, especially through writing, the dots become a part of common reality. And so we are saved.

It was left until the advent of "Walt Disney is God" that a certain secret was to be revealed, what we started with in this document: Judas volunteered. This was of the Mystery, the black dot that I was privy to, and that there was a certain danger to the Mystery being seen before the Knowledge. (The black dot, I am told, was just a legend in the secret society of Christians, actually a terrifying concept in what it was thought to hold, and discounted by some as being just a myth.) Now, since Judas is innocent, we have a serious break from the main doctrine of the Church. But what we have now are what is unlike anything former upon the world, something to which you can say, "Look, there is something new under the sun!"

If the Mystery were to have been seen before the Knowledge, it might in fact have been misinterpreted as the Knowledge. But understand that it is not the Gnosis. It speaks of the Mystery of that which is, that which was, and that which will surely come to pass. Glory to the Living God in Heaven and His Son, Jesus Christ, who is the Alpha and the Omega, the Beginning and the End. Blessed be the Holy Spirit, the Lord, the Giver of Life. Amen.

Sanity often seems like one is breaking the rules.

The question comes to Job (from the Book of Job, natch), "Where were you when I laid the foundation of the earth? ... when the morning stars sang together and all the heavenly beings shouted for joy?" (NRSV) So going back to the point where I overheard that Lucifer was the creator of pain: that would make none of our woe from God, at all, wouldn't it? Yet He makes no mention of Satan to Job. He basically takes all the blame for his troubles. Could it be like this for all the suffering that happens in the world?

One has to think that though God is omnipotent, that His brightest angel would still have been a handful if he were to rebel and turn a third of the angels to his side. Angels have perfect knowledge, and so, in seeing where his actions led, Lucifer must have concluded that he was going to *win* when he undertook to become Evil. Else he would not have done so.

Suddenly you would have had heavenly (read: *very* powerful) beings without any rules, grabbing for whatever power they can get their hands on, wreaking as much havoc as they could along the way. It would be a BIG DEAL. Victory would lie on a razor's edge, so faint it would have escaped Lucifer's notice. And because God is not the type to wave His hand and magically make things right again, this was real and true *danger* to all creation, through all of time. Remember, the Lord *watched* all 13.8 billion years pass before He came down to our sphere: this is not a hand waver. There is a certain magic to how He does *everything* (also we who serve Him), but it is the magic of work. God is love, *not* magic, and not luck. But know, as He knew, that we *do* win.

So if the Gospel is wrong about Judas, why should we believe any of it at all? But to the serious inquirer, this kind of question predates the revelation about Judas. Some lose their faith when they find out that a childlike belief is not one that is supported by the most basic scholarship in the area. One thinks as to how the New Testament came to be in the first place. Notably, it was made of "books" that resonated with many of the populace, which seemed to help one the most make it through this life. No esoterica; those books that were obscure, which only were read by the fringe — these did not make it in. Nonetheless, we also do not believe that the Gospels — and other books in the New Testament — were written by whom they claim is their authorship. That was never a prerequisite for their inclusion in the canon. So what are we to believe?

Well, to bring in a relevant topic, why it is that people say to learn the rules and then forget all those rules you learned: it is not to be in the same state than one who never knew the rules at all. People forget that Picasso, early on, did realistic depictions in his paintings. That's knowing the rules. Then he basically went to a place that the rules do not go. Learning the rules exercises certain muscles, whether they be bodily or purely mental. At that point you're supposed to rely on the muscle memory when you do your thing, which is to say, the "rules" are then thought to be digested, and indeed, have become part of one's gut instinct. Basically, automatic. You don't get that when you never learn them. But remember, forgetting them is the trick. Because now, with those well developed muscles, you can test the limits of what is possible: the boundaries known, from which one may break free.

So, how we deal with our problem of belief: first, familiarize yourself with the trappings of the faith. This is learning the rules. Pray, read the Bible, go to church. Get that muscle memory good and primed. One might believe that this is not all that is required for God to implement the new covenant in you, but it couldn't hurt: recall, He is to write His Law in our very hearts. Once we have accepted the Holy Spirit, the Lord, the giver of life, at that point, we are safe to break the rules. To go beyond what we learned, if we must. And we may then go back to the scripture that aided in our gaining of faith, and question certain things in it in accordance with our heart: this is to follow the inner voice. If you have not started down this road, may I suggest you begin your journey with, "God is love"? For love is the Narrow Way. And we are all of us made in the image of love, to have the Mystery in hand when we choose to love: because we all have wings, but some of us don't know why.[xxii]

What logic can be gleaned over the great swath of spiritual phenomena observed and reported? Is there any? Surely how the spiritual world is is unlike how things happen in the physical world; even two people of the same religion will see very different landscapes, while both claim to have true vision. If we take some sets of visions as having reality, say, from the prophets of the Bible, can we form a theory to how things just might work in this "unseen" world? What if the idea of form, the most basic of substance, is fundamentally different? What can we think of as true? For many come and go telling us of how we may view the events that occur in that world, and many are false teachers, only a few shall we hold as having been sent by the Most High.

Surely, that which actually relates of something in another place and/or time in the physical world, then means some reality must be accounted it. We can only hold that vision of the unseen world to be true when it has ground in the world that is seen. Even *if* the world that is seen is only temporary, and what is unseen is eternal. The Bible itself says what a prophet may claim must have basis in the physical world to determine if he is true, and so his visions come from God, instead of his own imagination. Perhaps it is the only indicator that whatever else the prophet says is true. If not, we have no obligation, and in fact, no basis to believe. And I think God lets it be known that this is the only trust.

Before I forget: Jesus *is* the Christ. This became evident to me only after years of Him banging his heart against this mad bugger's wall.[xxiii] I had been in communication with him since 1991, but I was going through a massive messiah complex at the time, so whatever clues were dropped my way, I either ignored them or denied they said anything at all. As far as I could tell, what my psyche's area where these visions happened, the HALOSPACE, it was like a land overgrown with wild, weedy notions, from what I had built as a subconscious through the years. Basically, his standing was beneath me in my mind, in that SPACE, so the Lord worked his way up. I remember him being on his knees, praying, for what looked like months. Eventually he won me over, and now I proudly say he is King over any space where I am. I owe him everything.

Only after I truly believed did all the clues make sense. When I remember my looking through his point of view, and the fact that *he never makes a mistake, ever,* and can in fact solve every mathematical problem you can pose him (if he feels like it, he doesn't have time to suffer *every* fool), can predict what's going to happen to the dot, never lies, and can call Superman a wimp, and has an infinite IQ (if that has any meaning to you), and has told me about that light of God I saw that he *is* that light (which I was told I am not, by that light) — then what you have, my dear friends, is the *literal* Son of God, in the only job that is fit for him: messiah. That's what Christ means, literally, "the anointed", which is another way of saying "king". He is KING OF KINGS, AND LORD OF LORDS.

Being in that position, what he really wants from us is not the grasping in the air of a simpering weakling barely holding on, but at your strongest, to give him your full allegiance. Remember, between what he'll take and what he wants spans an incredible range of human disposition. Sometimes he'll let the world turn you into a complete wreck, so you'll learn what humility is. And that's important, being the opposite of pride (the sin from which all sins come). *Only in that way* will he take you. And he'll acknowledge even the faintest "yes", but what he wants is... well, he wants it all. For you to hold nothing back from him. For you to give him mind, body, soul, spirit, and strength. But why would you possibly hold anything back? If one were to trust one thing — even more than oneself, if it be possible — it is to trust the Lord Jesus Christ. This is the clue to life.

Love is truth. What is love? If the universe existed and there were no love, would we all live in shadow, in Hades or Sheol, the ancient realm of the dead. I have some experience with what such a world might be like. Like I told you about the night I ended up in the hospital, I seemed to be in a dimension where some of what makes things real had been sucked away. I imagine the netherworld of old would have been that to the nth degree, void of light to the point of the dimmest gray, which is the color of Limbo.

What is real? To you? How much, how far, will we succumb to the illusion, of material riches and numbers on the bottom line: gold, supercars, mansions, yachts: not even that we should own them, but to drool over them, and how we envy the people who "have"? Love is free, dear child, and it is all in all that *can* mean anything in the whole wide world, all that can *give* meaning to anything. We will find that the ground of being itself owes its very soul to love.

What is love? For if you think that love comes cheap, you mistake a van Gogh for a chewing gum wrapper. If you think to have power is to have power over love, you are sorely wrong. For you cannot buy love, you cannot force love, you cannot cage love. Love would rather die than that another should have power over it. The best definition I've found so far of what it is: Love is give, and not take. That phrase is a wonder. And it's from the schlocky '80s movie *Electric Dreams.* Funny where is hidden the fathoms of wisdom. Such is love.

Every once in a while, a little of someone else's world opens up, enough to take a peek in. You can see for a second a glimpse of that person's problems, his worries, get a sense for what is important in his life, what's pressing on his horizon, even what things he pays no attention to. You may not know this person at all, but for that little while where you look in, whether through some phrase that slips out in an email or a mention in a phone call, that person is a person, just like you. You relate. You two may be living different lives — completely different lives — but you are both living lives; you both are fully human beings. The window doesn't stay open forever, and perhaps that's a good thing, because I think we do not have room to live more than one life at a time.

I sometimes think about such windows when I hear about death on the news. When I hear of some number of people being killed in some sort of horrible occurrence, man-made or otherwise, I think about how all these windows have closed for good.

The numbers do so little to convey that for each one of these within the statistics, there was a life there. There were years of experience, good and bad, that that person went through, digested, handled, folded and stapled. And there are years, now, that such a person would have gone through, but have no chance of doing so now. But here, too, such thinking is fleeting. We have none of us hearts large enough to handle the true total of tragedy in this world, or even that we hear about. We move on, thankful for the glimpses.

We of the age of television and video, even radio, should take heart in this phenomenon, of windows into other places, places just as real as ours, our own homes on this great earth. What did our Lord say, and what does every religion say? "Love your neighbor as yourself." Use your minds, use your hearts, see from the window cracked open before you that you and they are the same animal, and sometimes, the same angel. Everyone you meet is your neighbor, and you can see this when you do get the chance to look through these windows. That your homes are not the same, but you both have homes, that your hopes and dreams are different, but you both have hopes and dreams. Because sometimes, we are lucky enough to get the first commandment for free, "Love God", when we love our neighbor as ourselves. No deal better than that.

Remember: there is no question, love is the answer. Recall: the secret is love, tell everyone. The Mystery surely is so simple that we never truly grasp it. The way that beauty manifests in this world, what we all react to, what we all long after: it is hidden in the everyday, as Blake described everything being infinite in its true form. And you do *not* want to exist in a state of constant satori, please understand, so we deal with the averages. The Mystery is known in some circles as the Tao, and others as Brahman, and as the Godhead, and as transcendence itself. It itself has no power, but by it may you approach the Knowledge, the Certainty, and the Power of love. The only danger is that you may lose yourself in it.

The ordinary hides its sublime beauty in the disguise of the obvious, for even in the repetition is the triumphant of energies. Sift sand through your fingertips and into your other hand, and feel the luxurious dance of particles in fleeting moment imbue the sensation. And how are we, who are greater than sand, to make one another feel, not just by touch, but by faculty that sands do not possess? The Mystery is to find the Way that one should live, which is not one way, but Freedom. Why are we here? Animals are here to reproduce; and if we may turn that setting up an order of magnitude, we are here to *love.* Like all emergent phenomena, we the individual issues that are comprised of such a high coalesce societies ants could never dream of. The Mystery is no mystery. The Mystery is love. It is what makes the difference.

There are people who do nothing but complain. What are we teaching our children that they become that kind of adult? We recall that as children we did not appreciate that we had a roof over our heads, three square meals every day, a comfortable place to sleep, clothes enough for all the days of the week. The things we *had* to do, whatever they were, either we complained about them or accepted them in sad resignation. If we have children, we see the other side of that equation, as providers of that roof over their heads, those clothes on their backs.

Now, shall we also regress, to think along the lines that "in a perfect world", things would be different? Or do you invoke the Serenity Prayer, and do you change the things you can, and accept the things you cannot? For I speak not to these latter, but rather those former: would you rather to complain that to change something is too much work, or that the system is rigged, or that nobody is as unlucky as you — is it everybody's fault but yours? Will you have none of it when someone explains why for something, when it does not fit into "how the world works" according to you?

Are you not thankful for the ground under your feet, the air you breathe, water to drink, an entire civilization that supports your existence? For if you are reading this, you are more fortunate than most of the people who have ever existed. One needs to think about that. When we grow up, we should no longer be as the child who does not appreciate what the parent provides for them. I would suppose that it is harder to be thankful when one does not believe in a Provider above all others. But I say that there are believers who are ungrateful, too, and atheists who do appreciate all the universe holds. And if these are truly grateful for all that is, for their very lives: to them I say, you are not far from the Kingdom. For some have God in truth already, but just don't know it — just like an idea in the heart they have not the word for.

There is no truth in power, nor is there truth in money. Where do you suppose the truth is? The wise man will see both of those, the ruling and the riches, as necessary evils used as sparingly as possible to get things done in the world, and thinks it is better if possible to get things done without having to deal with either. It is too easy to get caught in the pursuit of one or the other, and often both together, and for a good man to lose his goodness by good intentions, to slip into the madness that sings so seductively: what he collects he would use for the betterment of all, but in the collecting makes room for that money and power by the squeezing out all remnants of his soul.

With power, one may believe that he can *make* truth by his own word or action; of course, this is an illusion, for to effect something does not create a physics. And he may find that reality will twist towards his own image or vision only so far before it snaps in two that which he does make. With money, one may think he can *buy* truth, but as you cannot buy love, with the truth it is the same: he may just find that he only buys the hollow forms that resemble what things in truth genuinely are. What power and money do get you, at the very best, is an artificial comfort. Yes, *that* not an illusion, but it is usually not what any soul actually longs for. Those who have one or both, money or power, are likely not going to be satisfied with so meager a prize, not when the world makes so big a production on how great is the ruling, how great is riches.

Shall we not, then, engage with the world at all? To strive, while in the world, to be a success and to live within that society as a good person, not as a recluse who hides in the desert to be alone with his God? The Lord said to a rich man: to be perfect, that he should sell all he has, give it to the poor, and to follow Him. Is this the only way? Can no one live in the world anymore, to effect change in how things operate, to do the Lord's will to achieve the greatest outcome that may be realized *within* the hustle and the bustle? Can we be Heaven's agent in a world that is ultimately ruled by the Devil? Perhaps, then, only needing to remember, though this is crucially to be called to mind: power and money are to be used, and people are to be loved. Not the other way around. Hearken.

When it comes right down to it, when the Holy Spirit asks something of you, is it yes, or no? Even easier, when we are unencumbered by the weight of the world, when it is purely choice, do we say yes to Him, or do we say no? For the offense that we will not ever be forgiven for, what is termed blasphemy to the Spirit of truth, is simply that: to say no. This is a very controversial bit of scripture, when the Lord tells us of this, the unforgivable offense: to say a word against the Holy Spirit. Sounds incredibly easy to breach this regulation. At one point I thought it was so stupid that I said out loud that "the Holy Spirit is a piece of s#!t." If you were going to damn me for something that innocuous, that kind of Heaven was not for me. Then the Lord told me that it was simply to say, "no", and that made even less sense. No sense at all, until much later.

When there is no devil your shoulder (nor angel on the other), faced with a decision that is pure choice, pure free will, which way will you go? For if you say no to the Spirit of love, that part of you dies: for we are made in the image of love. But we know very few decisions are so cut and dried, free from the weight of the world. Not to worry, because God understands if somehow we cannot sometimes abide by the rule of love: these would be that which encumbers us in our choice, which I mentioned. You are forgiven, if within you something still holds true. It is when nothing true remains in you that you have died as a child of God. And it is well taken by God when you *do* have the weight of the world pressing against you, and you still say yes — it is thus how saints are made... Sometimes we to say yes and it translates wrong. And perhaps rather to say no to ourselves, than say no to love.

So how are we to read the Bible, if we cannot count on it being in totality free of errors? First, read the Bible. It is first and foremost a book of the worship of the God who made heaven and earth, who made us. A lot of it may not make sense to us, for a lot of it espouses a philosophy created thousands of years ago. There are things like God telling the Israelites to eradicate *all life* in a city: men, women, children, *even the animals.* Surely we cannot be expected to follow such dictates in this day and age? If God were to tell me personally to kill someone, I would have to decline. But for all that's "wrong" with it, there is much that is right: and this is why it continues to be a bestseller. For it is convenient to God as a method for Him to write the Law in our hearts, which comes with the new covenant. One may worthily begin to hear his inner voice thusly.

So when you do read the Bible, let it be known that it is an insane philosophy to be of the sort that takes every word of it to be literally true. When the Law is indeed written in our heart, we may gain the gift of discernment. It is those who do need to take every word as being infallible who lack the Spirit: the spirit of truth, the spirit of love. For God not only gave us the Bible, He gave us a mind, and He gave us a heart. There is reason upon reason to believe that the world is billions of years old, and was not created in six twenty-four hour days. That Adam and Eve were not the parents of us all. I will go no further in this vein, for if you cannot have faith except with the crutch of blind faith to the scriptures, there is nothing I can say that will make you leave your crutch behind, and stand, and walk on your own.

We must look upon the Bible as what is now known of it: not everyone said what the Book says they said, nor did they all do what they are said to have done, and not all things happened like it said they happened. Is there a simple formula to discover which is true, and which needs a more reasoned approach? The Lord told us what this is: love God, and love your neighbor as yourself. And if the first is interfering with the second, you're doing it (all) wrong.

So to make some more observation into the meaning of things, again to notice how much we take for granted, music we've covered, but then there's the subject of mathematics. Physics, more precisely. This is what Albert was talking about how incomprehensible it is the universe's comprehensibility. Does anyone find it a bit *convenient* that there are equations that can predict how things will behave in reality? It has made some people think that God is a mathematician at heart, though I believe differently on that matter. But how *eerie* is it that Newton's laws of gravitation so closely match how things behave, but then Einstein comes along, and we have an *even more* precise description of how things must happen?

The greatest gift to knowledge of the twentieth century is the sense of uncertainty — just before it, the Enlightenment had physicists thinking we'd figured it all out, just some trivial details remained to be found. How wrong we were. The universe seems to be profoundly weirder than we ever before believed it could be. And yet, we can make sense of it. You don't find that at all *peculiar?* It's almost like it makes sense of itself *to us.* There was one scientist who likened mathematics to archeology. It may seem like a strange comparison, as we like to think of math as being a strictly logical endeavor, but really, it's a matter of where exactly you're digging, in both sciences. Sometimes to make a fortuitous discovery, sometimes to dig for years and years and come up with nothing.

If you really think about it, not only has all of science just barely scratched the surface in the lines of inquiry that currently exist, it has yet to touch the conceivably infinite lines of inquiry that have yet to be discovered. Like that dim gold space that I had a vision of, that stretched (as far as I could tell) out without end, so is that which can be known about the universe. If God is God, as advertised, this world is stranger than we *can* imagine. Until we discover it.

When we do discover it, most likely, it will conform to some mathematics. It is utterly strange how closely the weirdest things in our world are explained by purely mental constructs. Why is it that math works so well, but doesn't, in fact, seem to be "it", exactly? What does that mean? To the faithful, *everything* speaks of the Creator, and to the unbeliever, no evidence is sufficient. Mathematics is its own landscape, hearkening to an archeological paradigm again. It is a land within a land, a universe within this universe. Perhaps why it explains things so well is that it exists within the world it is explaining. And perhaps it points to something more: an order above all the observed orders, that explains why it does, in fact, work. An order that pronounces the Logos. Just a thought.

Coming back to some nitty gritty: if you recall, before the last set of visions I had, I had had "episodes" before, when the visions basically took over my day to day existence. It usually onset by my smoking pot and getting off my medication. Not this last time, though: no drugs involved at all, not even as innocuous as the marijuana. And every other time, after those visions basically "had their way with me", I always seemed to come down from the heavenly heights — and all I needed to do to explain things was to say that it was just a trip, just my brain imbalanced of its chemicals, rational explanations. But then this last time, I know from this one, I'm never coming down. The genie is out of the bottle, Pandora's box has been opened.

In all the other times, I'd always been able before to discern the hallucination from the reality — but they went over the top this last time. On Mac OS X, in the upper right corner is a magnifying glass which, if clicked, accesses Spotlight, to search. I tried that and that didn't happen. I tried again, and no. It was so ODD. Instead of Spotlight, Dictionary popped up on the screen. And the angels gleefully let me know that they were responsible for it. I tried it a bunch of times. *Holy crap, this is real.* Then I bring up a directory listing window and I had it sort by name, and that was the most messed up alphabetical order I've ever seen! Weirdsort. Whatever you want to make of it, I know what I saw. It made me question just where I was, astral-plane-wise. Or if I were even still alive.

---

i am aloft, floating in a stream of information
the idea has been hiding in oblivion, dug out from creation
i have picked at the outline, careful not to break the metaphor
clumps of false equations lie all around me
i do not know to where i drift, but trust these currents
to where next i must excavate, sift through the unknowns
where i dig, i shake the dust of immortals

Does the world make sense to you? If not, you are among the vast majority. Sure, *our* world makes sense enough: wake up, go to work, they give you money, you buy things, find someone and make a family: if you want to see it that way, no problem, really — some will say that that *is* the world making sense to them. But look out the window, or better yet, watch the television, and there's a whole mess of stuff that begs to be sorted out. Why do bad things happen to good people? That is the classic case of the world not making sense. Life isn't fair. (Though that once, re-member, I did overhear, "What's unfair about life is that it *is* fair." See if it makes sense to you now.) Perhaps I've written in this general vicinity previously, enough so that you can tell what I'll be pitching your way in this field.

So, can you do it? Can you make sense of all the world, the universe and everything in it? Is that possible for a mere mortal to achieve? What if one can answer "yes" to that? Would you put your neck out there with the solution to it all? And not just the number "42" am I talking about. And if one *does* figure it out, can it be put into words, even? Is it some sort of transcendental va-por-talk that says sounds that seem like words, but don't quite behave like them? Perhaps some really do have eyes to see. Let me tell you for our part that Philip K. Dick and I are witnesses to all that was, all that is, and all that is to come. In the paradigm of the bare metal of Creation. As I've written, he laid down the groundwork (to the tune of some 8,000 handwritten pages), and I am here to make sense of things, based on those and other previous works.

Simply put, if one only is to see what is material, it is not to see the whole route of where destiny leads, for most if not all of the destinies of the people in the world. Everyone has a destiny, and this is necessarily a non-material thing. Destinies cannot be traded, like coins. If you see only a part of the puzzle and think that is all there is, you will never solve it. Thus to think that the world is inherently meaningless: because the meaning is not seen with those eyes that you are used to. And too, sometimes to think it makes sense because you see only a piece of the piece (where things work out), and you are only playing with toys, with hollow models of things. For to see the grandness is also to see all the tragedy and woe, and to know where these things fit, too. As the mote in the eye of God.

What if all the world, and more: what if it all *does* make sense?

Why is life so hard, then, if God is good? There is a method to this mystery, in fact, more than one. To quote from the movie *A League of Their Own*: "If it wasn't hard, everyone would do it. The hard is what makes it great." Life, though, everyone does do it, else they wouldn't be a part of everyone? Missing the point. It's that the hard makes things worth it, right? Climbing the mountain a different sense of things than landing there by helicopter? It comes to the same logic why things are imperfect: you *will* appreciate it more. You get more with less.

But back to everyone doing it: actually, no, not everyone truly does do it: not everyone truly lives. For things that require craft, the technique of years' experience tend to produce things that show the care used in creating them. And so it would be with life: one where everything comes by just snapping one's fingers, however much material treasure is accumulated, this is just not the same as when things are earned through the work. We are not to throw away the conveniences, but also not to stop with what comes easy; an easier environment is to raise the bar higher at what you must achieve in comparison. For a life not well lived is bereft of its meaning. It is unfortunate that some people choose exactly that, forsaking the hard. The meaning of life is how much you've loved living it. An easy life is easily a throwaway existence — and love, it might be said, is all the things you keep.

"Operationally, God is beginning to resemble not a ruler but the last fading smile of a cosmic Cheshire cat." Julian Huxley said that, and I can quite see his point, why it looks as it does. Right? What Huxley is talking about is that we used to think the answer for *everything* was simply, "God". Lightning, rain, sunlight — God controlled everything. Now that we've found the scientific connections and explanations, where is there room for God? Way back when, in Eden, He would come down to earth and walk among us, tell us directly what we should and shouldn't be doing. From that, in the generations to come, He would retreat, farther and farther up in His cloud, so that in these days, He is almost like a rumor rather than the Main Story.

Well, for my part, God *has* spoken to me, directly, though it was much of the time like unto the prophets of old, where true He spoke, but He spoke in riddles to me. I am no Moses. And you are now reading the book of my prophecy, what the Lord revealed to me, some directly, some I teased out of the Mystery.

What if God always was at a place we can never reach — namely, infinity — and before, the primitive means of understanding Him that He gave us were like an adult who stoops down to the level of a child? As the child learns more, he finds that the world is so much richer than he had ever thought before, and more mysterious. God's connection to the world seems more and more subtle not because He has changed, but that our understanding of everything has changed; ultimately that our purpose in knowing: it is to transcend knowledge... if one is ever ready for it, a pure perception then how God is beyond, beyond all things... and waits for us to comprehend the magnitude of earth and heaven.

True love is a love that is meant to be, beyond the imagination of all the storybook writers. It was never meant to be *for us,* one might posit, as if to be a Platonic ideal from which all other loves are shadows of it. It is pretty much understood that it has never once surfaced in the waking world, no Cinderella, no Snow White, not for real. We have grown to accept it, that's reality. A real-life prince is not like what the cartoons imply one is. There is no fairy godmother, and the pumpkin remains a pumpkin. Yet we will still seek it out, the romantics of us. Every once in a while, one of us to find someone with whom we think we have it: love, true love. Even if somewhere very far buried is the voice that says no, that actually isn't what we were talking about. (So what, right? Close enough.)

A love that is truly meant to be is the reward we all seek, but we will find that we on this world are involved not in the destination, only the journey. Along the way, we will find meaning here and there, and we will find love that is "meant to be," of a sort; but the meaning in true love, the love divine — this is stuff not to be comprehended while still within the sphere of the material. This world was not meant for that kind of crown. Only transcendent can such love exist, and it is too huge for the entire world to hold. Thus in the idea that there is a meaning of life: one believes, dreams that there is some formula or philosophy or poetry, but we will always be short of inventing one that is really satisfying. Because the meaning of life is in love's true fulfillment, and none of us will ever know it, in this world. Not to say in settling for what we get, here and now, that we are getting nothing. It's just that *there is more than meets the eye.* You'll see.

Eternity has revealed itself to me as if in a fourth spatial dimension, as best I could perceive it from the framework of a mortal, out of my third, or ajna eye. And I saw those who were trapped in the lower realm, those who would never (some, never again) touch the face of God. There was a time when I was with Albert, and the subject of Adolf Hitler came up (last time, promise). Hitler came to me, thinking I could save him based on my old delusions of grandeur, and I just looked away: "I'm not the savior." And it got around that he ran out of advocates. "He did not survive," the Lord broke it to Albert and me. The wages of sin is death. Never forget that. This earthly realm, all of its material: all of it shall pass away, along with those whom Christ does not know.

All I saw in the lower realm, the finite realm, were the faces of the dead. Of those living, those whom Christ gives life eternal to, time is limitless, and spent at one's leisure; for those cast from Heaven, and those among them born on earth who also chose that direction of destiny, they are as if trapped in a walled off sphere of the æthers, never (again) to reach out to Heaven. For they chose the finite, they chose to be of the domain of evil, which is not of any part of Heaven — shut from eternity, never to taint the holy realm, especially if they once had. They did it of their own free wills, and they are responsible for their actions. Some destined to the outer darkness, while they breathe, not to breathe of the air of paradise.

How strong is your faith? It is true that for beginners, we would like to nurture their faith in a friendly environment, not rock their boats too severely. But those who claim to believe, who say they have weathered the years in their faith, yet in truth, they have their faith rooted in flimsy foundation: we don't want you. If your faith rests on Creationist dogma, we don't want you. If your faith rests on marriage only defined between male and female, we don't want you. If your faith rests on a Jesus Christ who hates *anyone,* we don't want you. For if you do any of these, you are rooted in ignorance, and not faith. He told us a few things that we should do, if we truly believed, and I bring up again that He said, "Why do you call me, Lord, Lord, and do not the things I say?" Do we forget what these were, those things? It's just one word: love. Nothing else.

Understand, we don't want you who follow dogmatic ways because we were not told by Him to abandon reason and science, to abandon compassion, to abandon forgiveness for *anyone* who asks for it. To listen instead to your own prejudices. You adhere to the teachings of mortal men, and not the words of God. Why don't we forgive you for such things as you do? Because you do not ask for forgiveness, thinking instead you are right in hating in the Lord's name. Because you do not forgive others, you fools. For He told us to *love,* and you do not follow that commandment. There is more hope for a criminal than for you, for a criminal knows what he does is wrong. Have you not read? Have you not heard? God is love, and He knows His own, and His own know Him.

As I said previously, it is where in our souls we have said no to the Holy Spirit, these places are where we have died. And it actually takes only one such like that for us to technically be damned. For thus we become imperfect, resigning any infinite nature, and are therefore subject to death. This is of the Age of Iron. So how are we saved, any of us? With God, all things are possible. I have seen glimpses of a Purgatory: it is a place to let go of those spots where we died, to let that which is dead die and never again bring them to mind.

Remember how the Lord said, "If your right hand offends you, cut it off," because it is better to be one-handed than our entirety be thrown into Gehenna? Purgatory is exactly that. Where the holy fire burns away all sin, and burns off where we have died, and that once we are bathed in the river Lethe, we may enter Heaven true saints: without sin. This is the gift of God to us. This is the consequence of the Age of Gold. Nothing we can possibly earn, only that the love of God is so great that He forgives us, even though we are undeserving. For what shall we boast about? That we have done what we are told? Surely, if we do all that we are assigned, we must say, "We are unprofitable servants, for we only did as we were told." This is the salvation of the Lord: bend thy knee, and be saved.

I come not to reassure all who call the Christ, Lord, that their places in Heaven are certain. That you who profess with your lips that Jesus is the Son of God are surely written down in the Book of Life. The prophets spoke wisely to some out there, that they praise God with their lips but inwardly are their hearts inclined toward resentment. Do you not have eyes to see? You must not think like those in religious power, who toe the line of a strange messiah; that fellow cannot be the Jesus Christ I have met. Your righteousness cannot be like those who accept that things cannot change, that it has always been like that: the rich get richer, the poor get poorer. I think I must try to love as Jesus Christ loved us, and sing my song to the sinners, the Godless, the heathens, the pagans, the addicts, the perverts, the prostitutes, those who dwell in the darkness by choice or profession. And how will *you* love? How will *you* do God's work?

For my part, you may call me Saint Jude the Tuned In — the twin of Philip K. Dick, who is Saint Jude the Tuned Out — and I am patron saint of all gays, lesbians, bisexuals, transgender, trans-sexuals, transvestites, and all you other FREAKS out there. And no, I'm not gay, etc.: they do deserve a patron saint, and therefore, since I so have advocated their cause, the higher ups deigned to put that patronage squarely on my shoulders. And I am surely glad of it. Those who would malign these who are different, who give no effort to understand, your own excuses shall be ignored. What hope is there for you, who burn the bridges you yourselves must cross in the pathway of salvation? As you have judged, so shall you be judged. Love returns to its source, and so does hate.

I read in the book *A History of God* mention of a mystic text called *Shiur Qomah* (The Measurement of the Height), and the image that was invoked in the few pages where it is described left quite an impression on me. In the measurement of God, the basic unit is the *parasang,* which equivalent to 180 trillion "fingers", and each of those "fingers" stretches from one end of the earth to the other. Of course, it isn't supposed to be taken literally, but it puts into perspective the kind of scale we should be thinking in when we conceive of the Divine. (Surely this speaks of how blind may pride make of us, that any of us would put our own intellect as holding a better logic than how this speaks of the Most High. Yet every time we commit a wrong, we are doing just that.)

I had this image one day of the garment of Him, each thread the diameter of a world, and each thread composed down to nanometer scales, with images in motion down the thread in the cross section, which one could only view if one cut it open — and this, no one would ever do. These threads sewn together by the seraphim, the "burning ones" in such infinite elaborations to make the holy cloth as the raiment of the "I AM"... Heady. It reminds me of the prayer that declares not to think I am something, but instead to know I am nothing. We should heed such a humility, when faced with such possible glory of what may be, above. And we wonder why we do not understand the purposes of such a being.

Love is work. To those who don't think so, you have not known in reality what it is to love; perhaps you have only heard about it in fairy tales. And even in fairy tales there is a challenge that the prince or princess must undergo. Because this is an inescapable truth in the real world: love is work. Any parent, for one, knows how this is so. This is the world we are presented with. One realizes, however, upon certain milestones, that the work is worth it. If it were not so, that conclusion just might be the death knell of the human race, at least of civilization. But by the mercy of God, we do find meaning in the toil. Even though there may be many a time when we feel we are at the end of our rope.

Now, Satan did not realize what he was doing when he was contending with God on how things would turn out in the universe, and the world at large. For all his works of pure evil, he did not comprehend it: that his spoiling, his making a wreck of things made a worthy ground of creation. This being why things are as they are is in large part by that adversity. Without Satan, there would be no such thing as adversity at all, and many, many things that are present in our reality would have been only of academic value. When there was only Heaven, love was free, not work, "ask and it shall be given you". Everything was in synchronization, true love was like an everyday happenstance. Everything worked out, not just in the end, but moment to moment, and there was no thing like pain. Things were sheer *perfection*.

Satan's "gift" to all of us was that of imperfection itself. It was the *invention* of pain. This was the new thing that he thought was so great, the opposite of good. What the Devil did was that within creation, now love is no longer effortless, but instead, that love needs to work at whatever it faces. Love costs. That this invention of pain, that it is for the most part antithetical to our well being: *the dread negative.* God Himself must struggle to give meaning to *anything.* And God Himself must to *die* to be a sacrifice for His creation. And now, there is randomness rampant in the cosmos, disasters to kill and maim great swaths of population without thought as to who is deserving and who is not. At whatever random place you end up, life is ultimately *unfair.* No one gets what they deserve. And true love, the very meaning of life, is impossible. But this: *this* is a test worthy of the children of the greater God. *That* is why God let it happen. This is the new meaning of life, found each to his own in the struggle.

This is not to say that evil will ultimately be forgiven: it just shows how God handles adversity: it is with such skill that it *looks* like Satan is doing God's will. This is in no wise the case; Lucifer does everything in opposition to what he *perceives* is God's will. But the Devil ultimately struggles in vain. *You cannot win against the God who is love.* This is where the whole issue of pride comes in, that somehow, the thought was undertaken that the creation could somehow prove greater than the creator. Not Satan's way, can this be so. Evil *by its very nature* cannot sustain itself, much less a world.

In this world at large, Satan is its prince, for how else could he have tempted the Lord with all the world's kingdoms? This is a world where evil is easy, and good is hard. So life is the ultimate test of whom you belong to, your very existence the knowing: will you do the work that God intended for you, or will you go the path of least resistance, to follow only that which is easy, and what gives you advantage? The children of God know what the answer to that is, and we prove it in our surviving. We fight the good fight. We finish the race.

And so is this existence now become a worthy test to see who we are that are God's children, for us to prove ourselves worthy of the life we are given. The children of darkness, the Devil's own, shall they fail the test, and the wages of sin is death. But fear not, for it has been foretold from the first how you will choose. Courage, child. God is love.

FIN

EPILOGUE

I still believe in the human race (because that's the only race we have). (Once all other options have been exhausted) I know we will do the right thing. We will feed the hungry (as soon as we find out how to profit from it). (When there is no more point to it) we will stop waging war. We will learn to live with Mother Earth (because we are not completely suicidal). (By the grace of God) we will redeem ourselves to our children. We will make of this planet a home we can be proud of (for there will be outcry whenever we start going too far wrong from this task). (Like in AA, we will trust in a higher power to give us strength) ourselves to believe that the problems that we have can be solved. And we will stop thinking the Apocalypse is around the corner, to neatly fold everything up and throw it in the fire (for if you know what life is worth, you will look for yours on earth).[xxiv] (No, this is not the end) rather to believe that the Beginning is near.

We can report this new beginning because of the sighting of the Knowledge: possibly the most important milestone of salvation after Christ left the planet. After that, the end of the War in Heaven. Then the Mystery could be revealed. (The Mystery is love, as is the Certainty, the Power, and the Knowledge.) When the Knowledge was sighted, there was an overwhelming exhale in heaven and earth, and everything changed. When the War in Heaven was won, all things could then be told, without the overarching fear that one might be helping the enemy, if inadvertently. What this is, in the unfolding of the Mystery, is to say that salvation has been implemented in the world. And I am a witness to this, for I am the keeper of that Mystery.

The question is only a simple decision: do you believe? Is there enough evidence, presented here, for you to wonder if there truly are things in heaven above that are worth your attention? Can things make sense when there is a God in that heaven, or do you still believe that ultimately, things are meaningless? For I cannot make your decisions for you — no one but you lives your life. If you decide not to give it a chance, that there might be something more than what you can hold in your hand — if you say that what you can hold in your heart cannot be real, as well, it is not the end of all things. For no one comes to the Lord except they be called. And I still may look forward to seeing you in Heaven, unbeliever. And if you do believe, but only talk about it: watch out, for God can make of the stones sons of Abraham. It is all a question of love.

There come certain moments in life, when it is as if everything stops turning, and for that moment, you are doing right by God and the world, and all that is wrong is quiet, and faded in the background's background. When for that short space in time you understand how it is that God is love, with all that happens in the chaos of things and the violence of the malcontented. Do not think it is an illusion that these moments are, for it is the worry, and concern about lesser things, that is truly the illusion. The place where you find the presence of God is hallowed ground, wherever you may find it. The bush that burns and is not consumed. Like the heart that knows what it is to love.

The Purpose, in this far strewn world, of which science and faith are clues that lead the way, is to find the music that creates you, and dance in your heart.

Peace. Amen.

END EPILOGUE

APPENDIX: JUDAS ISCARIOT

When Jesus Christ was in the custody of the Sanhedrin, Judas Iscariot showed up, sort of at the side door, out of the blue. He said to them, "I sinned; I handed over to you an innocent man." [Matthew 27:4 NCV] And he threw the 30 pieces of silver they had paid him back at them. Innocent? Had he thought during the handing over that Jesus was guilty? One might believe he always believed the Lord to have been innocent. One imagines that when he was making the deal, that it was not foremost on his mind that they were going to have him killed. Did he actually think he were doing the right thing, those hours ago? I will contend that of all the mysterious motives for him to perform the act, there is one more likely than the rest: he had been told to do it, by Jesus himself. After Jesus was in their clutches, Judas lost his nerve and goes back to them, they so keen on snatching up our Lord. He had found out somewhat later that they meant to kill him, and so the rescue attempt, however ineffective.

As is the common thought, did he have a change of heart from the time he handed Jesus over to recognize what he had done was wrong? Which would mean he hadn't thought it was wrong before, and he did now. There must have been a good reason in Judas' head why he handed the Lord over, at least, at the time. Had he at that point with the kiss not been convinced Jesus was the Christ? It seems unlikely that anyone who had been there for all the miracles — who was one of the ones who had been sent out by the Lord to *perform* miracles in his name — unlikely that he would not think Jesus was somehow sent by God, in some degree divine or holy.

If this were so, if Judas realized Jesus were holy, then either handing him over was the right thing to do or Judas suddenly and inexplicably became evil. Or perhaps it had been building the whole time? Or was he evil from the first? (That one unlikely by most imaginations, unless the entire discipleship, leading to the "handover" and throwing the money back at them was the way, ultimately, to redeem an originally evil person.) Or perhaps he became jealous of Jesus' authority, and he was fixing that problem with a prejudice. ...except then, some hours after, he repented...

One is used to thinking of Judas as evil. We rail against changing a story that is *that* well known, that you know by heart. It is practically ingrained in you. You will reflexively fight to defend what you *know* to be true: gospel truth, right? But often in studying the myth, the ugly head of reality peeks through, to see things we might not have thought of at the outset.

There have been theories as to how this myth (the myth of Judas the Betrayer) formed, like how Mary Magdalene were made into a repentant whore. Which now is pretty certain that was not the case. So, this "Mary Magdalene effect" — what if it happened as the gospels were being gathered, and written down? And the myth of the betrayal of Judas made it into the canon, with some other questionable parts, and now we accept it as being part and parcel of the Truth?

People don't even think about it any other way but the way we were taught in Sunday school, the accepted story being so prevalent. But what if, instead of him out of nowhere turning evil, Jesus Christ himself told Judas to hand him over, for it was his time? It makes SO MUCH MORE SENSE. Jesus Christ had not chosen a bad egg, who was completely blind to his divinity. Judas volunteered to hand him over, when the opportunity arose. Why did it end up being told the way it was told, how we've come to know it? If you know any Bible scholarship, there's a lot in that grand text that became as it was by various competing forces. Much of Isaiah, for instance, is thought not to have been written by Isaiah. And Biblical infallibility? That it is useful in any matter of faith? Judas being innocent may be the greatest of the whole Bible in which when you see it as being wrong, it makes *no difference* in how we are to worship God. There are other parts, too, that we now believe are just incorrect. And it perhaps diminishes the Bible in thinking we cannot inject reason into it and have it survive the medicine. Faith should be stronger.

In reading the Scriptures, it strikes one as to how — sometimes — it is, if not inaccurate, *imprecise*. Like the Babylonian exile. Even if the exile being not exactly 70 years is not brought to scrutiny, there is stuff in there about Babylon being overtaken in kind of a cataclysm, which presumably would have immediately preceded the Jews being released. But Babylon, for a historical fact, did not fall violently. Isaiah 13:19 says, "Babylon, the jewel of kingdoms, the glory of the Babylonians' pride, will be overthrown by God like Sodom and Gomorrah." But that didn't happen. It is true the Jews were released, but nothing like how prophecy laid it down.

To which the enlightened Christian will say, "the Bible is not history." Yea, verily. I will state a commonly held scholarly belief: the writers of the Gospel had a certain agenda, each of them, in writing them. Their motives were not to provide the most accurate account of what had happened decades before they first put pen to paper. And they most likely did not accurately attribute those writings, either (John didn't write John). So what do we believe? One can yet find the message in the Gospels, even if they are not all fact, in fact. And that's likely what the Gospels were meant to impart: the Message. Of a man who was God but did not lord it over everyone, even if that's what they called him. Who came to serve instead of being served, who did not conquer but took the worst that the world had to give and still was able to love it all. And us all. Who asked God to forgive those who were murdering him, for they knew not what they did. How is it served by blaming one of his closest associates for a baffling betrayal? Is that account of betrayal perhaps the tip of an iceberg?

Let me start with something from scholar William Klassen. This is what study into this area tells us: Judas = Judah = Jude = where the term "Jew" comes from. It was a time when Christianity was turning from a Jewish base to a primarily gentile following. In moving away from the jurisdiction of "the Jews" as the later Gospels call them, the followers become anti-Jewish, pro-Roman, to the point where in their "good news", "the Jews" cry out about their King... really? to crucify him, and further, "His blood be on us and our children!" And Pontius Pilate — who was removed from office at a later point for being excessively vicious — he was actually the good guy! Washing his hands of the whole affair (a Jewish gesture). One cannot look at this critically and not see something very wrong with this picture.

So, it was who that crucified the Lord? The Jews? Even if, as a rule, the Jews did not crucify anyone. The Jews, represented in singular form by Judas, the convenient prototype, who is in fact named so prototypically. That we don't now associate Judas with Jews in general anymore does tell us that the point of time is past the limit of relevance, and it may be now to reevaluate what exactly we believe and why. Because we understand that many constructs within the Bible are now antiquated, and some things have to be most severely interpreted, warped from their original positions, to make sense currently. We do not stone to death someone who has blasphemed anymore. And as for the New Testament, am I taking crazy pills, or does the text not at least imply the thought that Jesus Christ was coming back real soon in relation to those first-century disciples? We interpret that away, don't we? These are those warpings. We have grown used to them.

Judas has become a device. Once again, we look to Mary Magdalene. How convenient that we have a fallen woman that the Lord had turned from her wicked ways. But as we come into the future, we may find that the figure of Mary Magdalene may be rehabilitated, if the actual person never needed such saving as was thought. Judas is another matter. His position among the damned we learn from the mouth of the Lord himself, as (part of the) "gospel". Why should we believe differently, could that truly have been so wrong? Well, if you found out that the past did not happen as the Bible said, do you still believe that part of the Bible? I mean, factually. If your answer is yes, I can only shake the dust from my sandals and bid you good day.

"I sinned; I handed over to you an innocent man," he said. Why do we so desperately want a villain? The most foul one imaginable, one in the inner circle who turned evil, like the Lucifer myth. But then, let's say that Jesus had told Judas to turn him over, why does he try and rescue his master? Perhaps like the other disciples scattering at Gethsemane the night before, without the Lord, he lost his nerve. He wanted his teacher back. If he were, in fact, guilty, why would he not have run away? Instead, he shows up, out of the blue, and said as if confessing, "I sinned." I have done something wrong, I know it. This couldn't be what he actually wanted. "I handed over to you an innocent man." I am telling you, me, the one who gave him to you, this cannot be the plan: you do not put an innocent to death!

The Lord had said he was going to be turned over, but his disciples did not understand. Peter took him aside and told him not to speak of such things. The Lord said he was going to be handed over to be crucified, but that thought had not hit, just yet, when Judas identified him with a kiss in the darkness. Without the Lord, when Jesus Christ let himself be taken, the disciples were at a loss as to what to do. They fled. Peter would follow the ones that had taken him, but ended up denying him three times in his course.

Surely all this could not have been what was supposed to happen? The reality of it was so different from the words that had described it. They had been in his presence when he spoke of these things, and without him was gone all courage, all reason, all sense.

"I sinned; I handed over to you an innocent man." He repented, as if he had needed to. This was courage, do you not see? But it is written: he was a villain. You can say what you want, but what a billion say is truth, the whole truth, and nothing but the truth — how can you argue with what is there in plain black and white? The simple fact? You can't. But you can know better. Just like you can see that the story of Adam and Eve didn't actually happen like that, you can see that Judas is blameless. Because it makes no sense, the conventional story. He was Judas, Judah, Jude: a symbol for "the Jews", who killed our Lord and Savior. The death story of our Lord has suspect things throughout it. Will you not accept the spirit of the story instead of holding on to the letter? Perhaps now, we can be trusted with that canniness, to go in the direction the Bible is pointing toward, in spite of all that's wrong with it. If you don't think there is anything wrong with it, *read it.* We as a people did not remain unchanging in how our heart reacted and reacts. We found, and continually find, what is the good and what is the better that we can make of this world. Open your eyes/have eyes to see. Forgive everyone. Yes! *Forgive everyone!* For if we do that, it doesn't even matter who is innocent or guilty, right? Right? And it's not ours to judge, anyway. Right?

END APPENDIX

APPENDIX: THE MACHINE

There is a phenomenon we have all experienced, and most of us have not, for the most part, been able to name. I call it the MACHINE, and it is the face of the BLACK IRON PRISON as it is visible to the common eye. Philip K. Dick expressed it as, "The Empire never ended."[xxv] You can see it too: whenever someone follows the rules in cold calculation; blind to all but the exacting of the regulations; where instead, compassion could be shown: this is the action of the MACHINE. They let a piece of their soul die rather than to have a heart. This is how it proliferates. This is where we die, as black iron infuses our blood.

It is the mechanism of LAW, over LOVE. That being by which, according to the Apostle Paul, we are damned by brute, efficient justice. This is "just following orders". This is us standing by because we were told not to interfere, when evil happens right in front of us. And we know we can do *something*. It is the opposite of the Golden Rule, to follow the printed word rather than to feel for our fellow human being. It is the remnant of the Age of Iron, where such things as live sacrifice was necessary.

You can see it in everyday transactions. Where instead of being a human being, they forego humanity to become one with the mechanistic cold calculations of the Black Iron. Something simple like not letting someone pay $3 instead of $2.50 on a cold January night — just because the rules say you can't do that. You know what? This is the one time I'll swear: FUCK the rules. Be a human being. This is to say that being "only human" can work in the other direction, too. May it be that you are "only human" and have a heart. Why would you rather choose death over life?

As Philip K. observed, to fight the MACHINE is to succumb to such mechanistic process, because its nature is violence. (If you fight the empire, you become part of the empire.) To become one and the same with it is a living death. This is why the Lord told you how properly to deal with the MACHINE: love your enemy, turn the other cheek, pray for those that abuse you. This is how the Lord ultimately defeated it: He let it win. This is the mystery of the crucifixion. Because the MACHINE is not God, and knows not from where things come, nor to where things go. It is the

Lord who is the Alpha and the Omega, the beginning and the end. What the MACHINE lets go of, the Lord picks up. And it is not in all things: split open a piece of wood and the Lord is the one who is there.

Heed this advice: whenever you can give someone a break, do it. God is watching, and He'll remember all those little things. If you need rules, let love be your rule. This is the path of life. For by becoming part of the MACHINE: this is what it means to die. Not of body, for even though what is given to us in form is precious, God made you from the dust, and can make you anew when you return to dust. It is our temple, but we know that what we are, what is truly our life, is in the decisions that we make: so out of which font do you draw your inspiration? The narrow way, that leads to life, or the broad gate, that leads to destruction?

Those who say that they are Christians are not magically immune to the machinations of the MACHINE. In particular, those who say that they are followers of the Lord but are such as Fundamentalists, who hold to the letter of the Bible, so it is then that they die by the word. For the Way is not the Bible. The scriptures *speak* of the Way, and they *point* to the Way, but salvation is not the words of the Bible. It never has been. Before there was a New Testament, all that being Christian was were the questions, "Do you believe in Jesus Christ, the Son of God, risen from the dead?" and "Have you received the Holy Spirit?" That's it. The Way has always been in Christ, and what did He tell us was that Way? Love God, love each other. This instruction given by the Scripture overrules the Scripture. It is how one *defeats* the MACHINE.

Remember that most falls from grace do not happen from one grand gesture, but small whittlings on our souls. Remember that there is always a line you should not cross, for if you cross it once, twice, enough times — then that line is gone. This is what it means to be lost to the darkness. It begins and ends with your choice: choose life, instead of the mechanism that is death. Do not think, "it is a little thing" and decide unwisely; think instead to start small in the positive. If you have not yet, *start*. Today. For there is no other day than today!

END APPENDIX

ENDNOTES

[i] Lennon/McCartney, "All You Need Is Love"

[ii] Roger Daltrey, *Quadrophenia*

[iii] William Goldman, *The Princess Bride*

[iv] Steve Winwood, "While You See a Chance"

[v] Neal Israel, *Real Genius*

[vi] William Goldman, *The Princess Bride*

[vii] John 10:18, NKJV

[viii] Gottfried Leibniz, *Monadology*

[ix] Lennon/McCartney, "All You Need Is Love"

[x] William Shakespeare, *Hamlet*

[xi] Gary Zekley/Mitch Bottler, "Superman"

[xii] Joseph Heller, *Catch-22*

[xiii] William Shakespeare, *Hamlet*

[xiv] Douglas Adams, *The Hitchhiker's Guide to the Galaxy*

[xv] Emily Dickinson, "This is my letter to the World"

[xvi] Daft Punk, "Harder, Better, Faster, Stronger"

[xvii] Fabio Almeida de Oliveira/Ian Duarte, *Dark Side of the Moon*

[xviii] Michael Jackson, "Man in the Mirror"

[xix] 1 Thessalonians 5:21, NKJV

[xx] Mick Jagger, "2000 Light Years from Home"

[xxi] Revelation 13:8, NKJV

[xxii] Michael Hutchence, "Never Tear Us Apart"

[xxiii] Pink Floyd, *The Wall*

[xxiv] Bob Marley, "Get Up, Stand Up"

[xxv] Philip K. Dick, *VALIS*

Printed in Great Britain
by Amazon

78866163R00079